The Pilot's Voice

Words of Warning to Youth and Enlightenment for Parents

Isabel C. Byrum

The Pilot's Voice: Words of Warning to Youth and Enlightenment for Parents

Copyright © 2023 Bibliotech Press
All rights reserved

The present edition is a reproduction of previous publication of this classic work. Minor typographical errors may have been corrected without note; however, for an authentic reading experience the spelling, punctuation, and capitalization have been retained from the original text.

ISBN: 979-8-88830-447-1

CONTENT

Preface iv
Chapter I   The Ocean of Life 1
Chapter II   Leaving Port 4
Chapter III   Misty Weather 18
Chapter IV   In the Tide 32
Chapter V   Danger Signals 43
Chapter VI   The Shoals 52
Chapter VII   Stranded 61
Chapter VIII   Shipwrecked 70
Chapter IX   A Light in the Distance 76
Chapter X   The Life-Line 84
Chapter XI   A New Voyage 88
Chapter XII   Anticipations of the Journey 96
Chapter XIII   The Pilot's Work 103
Chapter XIV   The Life-Preserver 111

Preface

Many books have been written for the instruction and enlightenment of the youth of our land, but there is still a need for more. In this day and age, when there are so many unwholesome stories afloat to mislead and corrupt the immature minds of our young people, we should do all that lies in our power to counteract the influence of such dangerous reading material, and to help youthful persons to understand themselves and to be able to judge between right and wrong principles.

All the characters mentioned are real, but their names have been changed, as some of the persons are still living and do not care to be so publicized. The object of the story has been to help youths as they start out upon the Journey of Life for themselves. Byron's experience will help them to see the necessity of being piloted by the One who understands the dangers abounding in the great, broad ocean before them, and will direct them to the Holy Spirit, who alone is able to serve as Pilot. The remindings given by the conscience will show how necessary it is for all to have a higher and a greater power to guide them through the tests and temptations that assail mankind. But it must have the cooperation of the Holy Spirit in order to be able to perform its work properly.

How often we hear someone say, "If only I had been taught concerning the fruits of disobedience, how many sorrows and heartaches I could have avoided!" Many lives that could have been bright and happy is sad and blighted by the effects of sin and disobedience. This simple story will fulfill its mission if it helps honest souls to listen to the warning of "the Pilot's voice."

—Isabel C. Byrum

Chapter 1
The Ocean of Life

The warm and sultry day was drawing to a close. Long shadows stretched across the countryside. The lowing of cows waiting to be admitted into the barn-lot could be heard, and among the honeysuckle vines the dull droning of bees told that their labor for the day was nearly ended.

Down the dusty road in the gathering shadows a lad of sixteen summers was hurrying along. One could plainly have seen that the boy was from a good home; for his clothing bore the marks of a loving mother's care, and his brow was high and noble. In his countenance there was a frank and open look, but his brow was drawn as if he were in deep thought, and a close observer could have detected a look of unrest and guilt. Now and then he looked behind him as if expecting to see someone coming. He had a long way to go and was anxious for a ride. No one being in sight, the look of expectancy in his face gave way to that of disappointment.

At the crossroads, after looking in each direction, he stood for a moment trying to decide what would be best to do. "By cutting across these fields," he reasoned with himself, "I shall save much time and strength." He was soon over the fence that surrounded the pasture and speeding across the rich meadows. He did not stop to look toward the large barn at his left nor toward the farmer nearby calling to his cows. The boy was known and respected by the farmer and he knew that crossing the meadow would not be accounted as trespassing, and this evening he had no time for conversation or delay.

He soon reached the other side of the pasture, and climbing the fence, he entered a field through which a small creek was flowing. Many times he had played along the banks of this stream with his little brother and sister, and the pleasant memories of strings of fish and little frolics came before him. For a moment he hesitated, looking down into the sparkling water to see if a fish was in sight. Then he hastened on.

Coming, at last, to a shallow place, he sprang from one stone to another and soon reached the opposite bank. He sprang lightly over another fence and passed through a large cornfield, keeping between the rows of knee-high corn. He entered the woods on the other side, following the path that wound in and out among the great oaks and maples. On and on he went, until he came to another stream—a deep river, somewhat swollen by recent rains. The boy, familiar with the whole area, knew of a foot log a short distance away. He realized, however, that the log would be slippery and that in the deep shadow of the forest he would have difficulty in crossing even with the aid of the handrail. But he had no time to go to the bridge farther up the river.

As he stepped upon the log, a strange feeling of fear and dread swept over him. The water beneath appeared so dark and chilly. An owl hooted in the distance and caused him to start; then a whippoorwill began its evening song, and he trembled.

"What is it?" he asked himself. "I am no coward! It must be the stillness of the evening and these darks woods that cause me to feel so strangely!"

Again he cast hurried glances up and down the river, and, nearing the center of the stream, he stopped to listen. All was silent save the river. He could hear the rushing and swirling of the waters below the rapids a short distance away, and he heard something else.

The voice of his conscience was speaking to him. It was warning him in almost audible tones of the dangers that he might soon meet if he continued his trip. This voice was also giving him hints of the future if he continued to follow the course in life that he had chosen.

There were many dangers ahead of him—dangers that in his own strength would be very difficult, if not impossible, to overcome; dangers that would need an experienced eye to detect and that would wreck his soul if he had no Pilot to guide him through the great ocean before him.

As he listened to the voice, the form of one he dearly loved arose before him. She, too, had warned him of danger and her words were still clear and distinct in his memory. Her warnings had been not only of the penalties connected with crime but also of the effects of sin and wickedness of every sort upon the human mind, body, and soul. And she had taught him how to avoid the errors that so often lead the young astray and cause them misery and sorrow. She had also urged him to make the right preparations before starting out in life for himself.

"The ocean of life is deep and wide, Byron," she had said. "You cannot cross it easily or in a moment of time. The other shore is safely gained only by those who understand the dangerous rocks and shoals, and who can brave the dangers of the deep. Therefore everyone should let Jesus, through the Holy Spirit, pilot him in this voyage that we all must take."

In fancy he could still see her near the gateway at home, begging him with tears in her eyes to change his plans for the night, and then, like a flood, came his own cruel words surging in upon him— "Mother," he had said, "I am almost a man, and I ought to have some responsibilities in life. I think I am old enough to decide some things for myself."

And then he seemed to hear again her answer, "My son! Oh, how I tremble for you! I am afraid that if you follow out your plans tonight you will fall into company that will do you harm! The boy that you wish to spend the night with is not the sort of person with whom you should associate. I cannot give my consent to your going. If you go, it is against my wishes."

And he had rudely answered, "Now, Mother, you're doing James an injustice when you speak of him as you do. He is all right. You can say what you please, but I am going anyway. You are always trying to tell me what I ought not to do, but I'm not going to be a sissy any longer. I'm going to take things into my own hands tonight and decide for myself. I won't be babied any longer! Here I have wasted an hour waiting for your consent. It's now past time for me to start! I should have been well on my way by this time. I shall not wait a moment longer to hear more of your argument."

And then his mother's farewell words repeated themselves— "Goodbye, my boy, goodbye! Remember, I shall pray for you tonight." He could hear the echo vibrating through the air: "Goodbye—pray—tonight—pray—pray—"

CHAPTER II
LEAVING PORT

Byron's mother was a Christian woman, and she knew the power in prayer. Often during severe trials and in perplexing times she had carried her burdens to the throne of grace. And as she poured forth her sorrows there, she always received strength and help that she needed.

For some months her son had, much to her displeasure, been associating with James. On the evening when Byron wound his way through field and forest, across the stream, and on to the place where he was to meet James, his mother's heart beat anxiously for her boy. When he had left her at the gate, she had watched him hurry down the road until he was hidden from her view. Then with a sad and aching heart she had turned and entered the house. The evening work was waiting, but she had no heart to do it. Entering her bedroom, she closed the door and, kneeling in her accustomed place, poured out her heart's sorrow in earnest prayer to God.

"O Lord," she cried, "Thou knowest the burden of my heart; Thou knowest that I must have Thy help and strength to bear up under this trial. I have done the best I knew to do and have used all the judgment Thou hast given me, in the matter. Byron has disregarded my wishes and advice. I am going to commit him into Thy hands, and I pray Thee to take care of him and help him to see the error of his way, and to save his soul. Send Thy Holy Spirit, Lord, to talk to him through his conscience, and pilot him through this night."

When the prayer was ended she felt relief and went about her evening duties, but her mind was still upon her son. Byron had never before spoken to his mother in such a way, utterly disregarding her advice and judgment, and his cruel words could not be forgotten.

A week before, Byron had arranged with James, a boy a year older than he, to spend Saturday night with him.

All week long he had thought of his promise, and each day had planned to speak to his mother about it, but his courage had always failed him when he saw her. So the entire week had slipped away and Saturday had arrived without his having gained his mother's permission to go.

At noon he had felt that the time had come. He must tell her, but how? He felt sure she would ask him certain questions, and how could he answer them? His mother had grounds for her poor opinion of James, for he did many things that were wrong. He had left his home in another state and for most of the way had stolen rides on freight trains.

For more than a year he had been living a few miles from Byron's home, at the homes of the farmers he worked for. He went to Sunday school in the same country chapel that Byron attended, and it was in this way that the boys had become acquainted. A few times he had returned with Byron to his home.

After one of these visits Byron's mother had talked seriously with him. "Now, Byron, I don't want to deprive you of associating with other boys. It is right and proper that you should do so, but you ought to choose good boys for your companions. I should like to have you associate with those whose actions you can imitate and who have a good, strong, Christian character.

"You are now at an age when impressions are being made upon your mind that will last all through your future life. You are now neither a man nor a boy, yet you have manly principles unfolding themselves within you. In other words, you are molding either a good or a bad character. You cannot associate with evil companions and not have their imprint left upon your heart. Like the photographer's camera, your heart has a sensor on which impressions are being made through exposure. When you are exposed to unclean or impure objects, is it strange that the heart becomes filled with thoughts that are evil? Is it strange that sinful acts are then committed? It is not strange, for Jesus said, 'A good man out of the good treasure of his heart bringeth forth that which is good; and an evil man out of the evil treasure of his heart bringeth forth that which is evil: for of the abundance of the heart his mouth speaketh.'

"The world, Byron, is as an ocean—great, deep, and wide—and all humanity must spend their mortal life upon it. God has so arranged it that everyone may choose his own course upon this great sea, but He desired them to follow the directions that He has marked out for them in His guidebook—the Bible. If they decide to follow His instructions, He gives to them His Holy Spirit as a Pilot to guide them by speaking through their conscience in every trial and difficulty through which they may have to pass. Should their course be marked by danger and trial, there will be rewards and victories as well, for these things belong together. If, on the other hand, a man chooses to depend upon his own judgment and the advice of companions who, like himself, have no Pilot, he will be guided into new problems. He will find that he has no idea what lies before him, and sooner or later shipwreck will be his doom.

"For this reason I cannot feel right about your associating with James too much. It is all right to treat him kindly and to try to help him to do right, but you will not be able to help him if you become close friends, for he will influence you in the wrong direction.

"He has lived among all sorts of people and has come in contact with sin of nearly every kind. You can see by his face that he has formed sinful habits that ought to be shunned. Just because he attends Sunday school and church does not prove that he is a good boy, by any means. It may be helpful to him, and no doubt it is. A religious influence is good for anyone, but the influence that he gives in return must be avoided. From the time I first saw him I have not liked his appearance. He never could look me square in the eye. He always has an expression of guilt that an innocent boy does not have.

"I have tried to be kind to him when he has visited you, hoping that I might be of some help in turning him from his sinful habits. But I see that my influence has not any good, and, sad to say, he is doing you harm.

"Ever since your father's death, when you were a small boy, I have felt the burden and responsibility of bringing you up to manhood with high and noble principles within you. I have tried to guide your feet in the right path. You are now at the most dangerous period of your life, when you need good, wholesome advice, and what I am telling you is for your future good.

"Now, James is older than you are, and you will unconsciously be led into company where it will be very hard for you to stand up for the right. Do you remember the account in your old school reader of the plateful of beautiful apples with the rotten one in the center?

"A father had noticed that his son was being influenced by evil companions. He decided to give him an object lesson, and so he placed a number of fine ripe apples on a plate. After showing them to his son, he put a rotten apple near the center of the pile. Then he placed them carefully in the cupboard and said, 'We shall enjoy them later on.'

"His son was quite surprised at this. 'Father, that rotten apple will spoil the others if you leave it there.'

"But the father paid no attention to his son's warning and closed the cupboard doors.

"Some time later the father called his son to him and said, 'Now, we shall get our plate of apples and eat them.' Reaching into the cupboard, he carefully took down the plate. But when they looked at it, they did not see the fresh, beautiful fruit that had been placed there. The bad apple had ruined the good ones, and none of them were fit to eat.

" 'Did I not tell you,' exclaimed the boy, 'to keep that rotten apple away from the others, or it would ruin them?'

" 'Yes, my son,' his father answered, 'I know that you told me, and I also knew they would be spoiled. Do you know why I put that rotten apple with the others? I wanted to show you that a bad boy is like a rotten apple and causes his associates to become like himself.'

"Now, Byron," said his mother, "think about the lesson of the apples, and about what will affect you. My daily prayer is that you may become a good Christian man."

Byron really wanted to become a noble and useful man in the world. So whenever he saw James at Sunday school after his mother's talk, he thought of her words. But as week after week rolled by, he tried to make himself believe that James was not so bad after all, and that his mother was just a little too careful and particular.

The daring stories James told him from time to time fed the restless nature within him, and, regardless of the apple story and his mother's advice, he longed to be with James as he used to. Still, he did not like to invite him to his own home, while his mother felt as she did. After many an argument with himself he at last silenced his conscience for a season and began to plan how he could have secret meetings with James.

Now, Byron had a cousin who was near his own age and who lived not far away; and as the cousin was a good boy and carefully trained by Christian parents, Byron was often encouraged to visit him. Satan was not long in taking advantage of this opportunity and soon helped Byron in his scheming by presenting a way whereby James could meet the cousins down the river. He also gave James the shrewdness to only lead the boys on a little bit at a time in things they had been taught were wrong. And if the boys doubted that it was all right to do, or if they were afraid of being found out, James would ridicule them and make them feel ashamed.

Thus the two cousins were given the impression that their home teaching was not the kind that would make them brave, strong, and daring. Many times they did things they didn't want to, that they might not appear cowardly before their hero. At these secret meetings the three would often go fishing or swimming. When the cousins suggested that their mothers did not approve of doing such things on Sunday, James would answer with a coarse laugh, "Yes, there you go again. Always quoting what your mother thinks. I wish you boys could remember that our actions are secret—no one's going to find out what we do, so don't worry about getting into trouble."

In spite of his efforts to forget them, Byron would sometimes think of his mother's warnings and of the apple story, but he would quickly banish such thoughts from his mind and endeavor to excuse James because of his lack of home training. But by now he knew that James was a bad boy and that his own desire to be with him and to do as he did was stronger than it had ever been before. He also realized that now, when James proposed doing something wrong, instead of saying that it was not what they ought to do, he was sometimes influenced to take part in it.

Byron told James how his mother did not want them to be together. James said, "Well, never mind, Byron. I know that your mother is a good woman and means well, but she doesn't understand as I do your desire to gain a knowledge of the world. What can you learn, shut up as you are at home on the farm away from those who know what real fun is? I tell you what, Byron, it will be a grand day when you are able to do as you please."

Thus Byron was encouraged in wrongdoing. As far back as he could remember, his mother had taught her children to gather together for a worship hour, and to bow with her in prayer. This he came to regard as tiresome and monotonous. The only part that he looked forward to with eagerness was the "Amen." In fact, many things that he used to delight in he now no longer enjoyed; especially was this true about his class on Sunday in the little chapel. His mind was not on his lessons any more. He spent the time thinking of the fun that he would have at the riverside when he was with James. He enjoyed hearing James tell of the many things that he had done—of his stealing rides on the trains from one town to another, of the dangerous exploits that he had done, and of visits to saloons and other places of wickedness—and wondered if he himself would ever do those kinds of things.

Whenever he thought of the disgrace that such a downward course would mean to his family, he would reason, "They would probably never find out about it." Thus the voice of his conscience was constantly hushed; and, without the Holy Spirit to pilot him through life, he was in great danger.

Upon a certain Sunday, when the three boys were together, they strolled back into the woods. Here, in a lonely place, they seated themselves upon a grassy knoll beneath a large beech tree, and James, whom the boys recognized as their leader, addressed them. "Boys," he said, as he pulled something from his pocket, "I have something here that will be of interest to you."

"What is it, James?" both boys exclaimed. "What have you got?"

"I have a pack of cards," James answered, shuffling them carelessly in his hands. "These are the kind of cards that are used by gamblers and in saloons. I learned to play the game when only a small boy and can say it is not only interesting but beneficial as well, as large amounts of money can be won when it is properly played. I have never mentioned it to you before, because I know how strict Byron's mother is about what he does or thinks, and I supposed she would be against this, of course. Now that you are becoming better acquainted with me and my ways, I shall tell you about the game, and," he added confidently, "I am going to teach you how to play it, for it is not hard to learn it."

James was dealing out the cards before the boys had an opportunity to say anything. Now Byron had played with the cards of the Educational series, but his mother had often warned him against the kind that the gamblers used. As he looked down at the cards before him, he thought seriously of his mother's words.

"James," he said with deep emotion, "I can't feel right in playing this game. I'm afraid my mother will find out about it."

"Oh, come Byron," James urged, "don't always be a boy! You are almost a man, and it's high time you were learning some of these things."

After a little of this kind of persuasion from James, the boys consented to learn and the game was begun. Now and then James made remarks about the impossibility of Byron's mother ever finding out that they had been playing cards, and about the many people in the world whose fortunes had been made by gambling. The fascination of the game, together with James' reassuring words, made it very easy for the boys to continue, and game after game was played, in which one or the other of the cousins was permitted to win.

So interested had they become that they did not notice that the sun was sinking fast and that the shades of evening were already gathering. Knowing that he would be expected home by sundown, Byron sprang suddenly to his feet, saying, "My, but the time has gone rapidly! I had no idea it was getting so late. That game is interesting, all right, and I don't like to stop playing. It surely can't be as bad as Mother has said, and I don't see why she should object to it. She probably has never watched a game of this sort played. She has been altogether too strict with me."

"I believe that you have a good mother, Byron," James said; "but there is no need of depriving a fellow of all the pleasures along the way. Why, we only pass through this life once, and we might as well get all the enjoyment out of it that we can."

The following two weeks Byron was kept so busy on the farm that he had no time for himself. When again the boys met near the river, a young man named George was with James. George, though not much larger than James, was older, and sin had left in his features deeper and harder lines. He stayed with a farmer who lived about a mile from where James worked, and the two boys were often together. The cousins found him to be a very jolly and talkative companion and were soon much interested in the stories he told them of his adventures. Then they all retired to the secluded place in the woods where James had produced the deck of cards.

During all the past two weeks of hard toil on the farm, Byron had not forgotten how much he had enjoyed the card game. Sometimes he wanted to talk about it to his mother and tell her how very interesting it was. But he always shrank from doing so when he thought of James' words—"They are what the gamblers use in the saloons"—and remembered about the large amounts of money he could win when he learned how to play. How he wished that she would approve of the game!

Now, as he seated himself upon the green turf and the older boys began to play, he again thought of his mother's teaching and heard the voice of his conscience speaking. But the game was so interesting that he soon accepted an invitation to join the others. For an hour or more they played, and as Byron became more and more fascinated with the game, he endeavored to learn all the little details that he could. He quickly many little tricks and methods by which he could take advantage of the other players dishonestly.

"Oh, this is too tame!" said James, after a bit. "Let's put a little life into it! Come, get out your money, Byron, and let's play for a small stake."

"Why, that would be gambling!" Byron exclaimed in a horrified tone, realizing how things were going. "My mother—" he continued, but the look upon James' face made him ashamed to finish the sentence. For several minutes he remained silent. "Mother has always said that gambling and card playing go together," he thought, "and here the boys want me to gamble! What shall I do? If I tell them no, they will call me a coward, and perhaps take my money from me; and if I lay it down, I shall stand a chance of winning it back and more." Hesitating, Byron slowly pulled out his wallet, saying, "What would Mother say if she should find out about this!"

"There Byron goes again, worrying about his mother," James said, and he laughed coarsely. "He is always wondering about her, but he's better than he used to be. He's becoming more manly and will soon be able to think for himself."

James' tone and manner when speaking of Byron's mother made Byron wince, and when James added, "Come now, old boy, your mother will never find out about this, so fork over your money like a little man," Byron's face became scarlet, and be dared not look up. James' rough words and manner had stung Byron to the very depths of his soul, and for a few moments he did not know what to do. He would have been glad to be at home. It was hard to stand such ridicule, and now that James was losing his reserve, Byron could see plainly that his mother was right in her warnings. But there was a fascination about it all that he could not resist.

As soon as he was able to do so, he tried to laugh and not to appear offended at the rough remarks. Then, fearful lest something more be said about cowardice, he counted out his money, finding that he had just forty-seven cents, and quietly laid it down upon the grass. The other boys soon followed his example. Each put down a similar amount, and then all were ready to begin the game.

The manner in which the boys received their money was somewhat different. James and George were paid wages for their work; but by the time they paid for their clothing, they had very little left for other things. Byron and his cousin did not have to plan for their clothing, as it was always supplied. Whatever money was given them they could do with as they pleased; but they had been taught to use it carefully and to make it go as far as possible. It was therefore with reluctance that all the boys had parted with their money, but each was hoping to receive it back again with interest. With this thought in mind, James said, "We will not make the amount very large at first. We'll each lay down a nickel, and the one who wins the game will receive all the nickels."

In the game that followed each player tried to do his best. Every card was carefully studied before it was thrown down, and the players tried to take advantage of the others in every way that they could. George won, and as he triumphantly picked up the money, James said excitedly, "Now, boys, we ought to have more money than this. None of us here have much to spend, and we ought to figure out a plan whereby we could get more. I asked my boss the other day to pay me higher wages, but he only laughed at me and said he was paying me now more than I earned. I should like to have several dollars to blow in every week."

"I agree with you," George added emphatically. "Money is a good thing to have, and the more we can get in our possession the better time we can have." Then he added in a lower tone, "I have been getting some extra of late, and I mean to get some more soon."

"How is that?" James asked quickly.

"Why, I've been finding some loose change lying around," George answered. "It's an easy matter to find it when you try; but, of course, you have to be very cautious and can only take a small amount at a time, but it's a help."

"Good for you!" James said, slapping his companion on the back. "That's the way to do it, and I guess it does help!"

An awful look of fear swept over Byron's features. He realized that he was a companion not only of card players and gamblers, but of thieves as well. Could it be possible! What would his mother say about it? He could almost see her white face and hear her saddened voice warning him against such a course in life. Could he ever meet her again?

Suddenly, however, he was awakened from his reverie. "Look here, boys," James was saying, "I have a plan all figured out, and I know it will work fine! Here is Byron. He receives no regular wages for his work, and he is entitled to a share in the things that are produced on the farm. He helps to produce them and ought to share in the benefits. Here is the plan: his mother has a large number of chickens, and each day he could lay aside a few eggs and hide them somewhere without their ever being missed. Then when he had collected a sufficient number, he could in some way manage to market them and thus secure a nice little sum for himself. And," he added with a meaning glance, "I am sure he would be willing to share up with his best friends."

"James, you are always full of new ideas," said George, approvingly. "I never would have thought of that plan."

Byron remained silent, more troubled than ever. The remarks made about his being able to securely hide things from his mother brought to his mind an incident that had taken place several years before. Thinking of this, he quite forgot that he was in the presence of the boys, and imagined himself back at home between the long rows of corn.

The incident occurred when he was about nine years of age. "Byron," his mother had said, "I want you to take these beans to the north cornfield and plant them in with the corn. There is no other place to plant them now, and they should have been planted before this. As they are a variety that grows very tall, they can wind around and climb up on the stalks of corn for their support. You may make a small hole beside each hill of corn and drop a single bean in every hole. I will not need your sister in the house today, and she may go and help you with the work. It will be best for each of you to have a small stick sharpened at one end. With these you can easily make a small opening in the ground, where you can drop the bean, and then you can cover it with earth."

Hastening to the woodpile, he soon prepared, by the aid of an ax and a jackknife, the two sticks. He brought them back to the house, where he found his sister waiting for him. In her hand was a tin pail that contained about four quarts of beans.

As Byron sat there among his friends musing, he remembered how beautifully the sun shone that morning, and how sweetly the meadowlarks were singing, as he and his sister walked to the cornfield. The sweet odors from the clover blossoms seemed again to fill the air. He remembered how, as they were climbing over the pasture fence, they had accidentally spilled part of the beans. They made sure to carefully pick every bean that had spilled. Then they eagerly made ready to start.

As they planted one row after another, their enthusiasm arose, and his sister remarked, "Say, Byron, this is fun! It won't take long to plant these beans."

"Yes," he answered, "it's more like play than work."

But after a while their ardor abated, and he remarked, "This is going awfully slow. The beans in my pail are disappearing so slowly I fear it will take us a long time to plant them."

"Yes, and my back is getting tired already," said his sister.

At the next hill Byron had accidentally dropped two beans instead of one in the hole that he had made. Just as he was about to reach down to remove the extra one, a thought flashed through his mind.

"Say, Sister, if we just drop two beans in each hole, we can finish our work much sooner than we shall be able to do at this rate."

"I know that Byron," his sister replied, "but Mother told us to plant only one in each hill."

"I know she did, but when shall we ever get done? No one would know about it if we dropped two in a hole, and we could do it just as well as not."

After talking the matter over, his sister agreed to plant two beans in each hill, instead of one. After they had planted a few rows in this way, there were still a good many beans left, and they were both getting very tired and hungry. So, in their eagerness to finish the job, they did not stop with putting two beans in a hole but often dropped in four or five. Yet, even though they were using up the beans quite quickly now, there were still a number left when they heard the dinner bell begin to ring.

Looking about him for a place to hide the remaining beans, Byron discovered a stump and said, "Here's a place, Sister, where we can hide our beans and make the folks think they're all planted. Come, let's empty our pails and cover the beans with a little earth. Then, if anyone asks us if we have planted them, we can answer yes, and no one will ever know the difference." With one accord they deposited the beans about the stump and after carefully covering them hurried to the house for dinner.

"Well, children," their mother asked, "did you get the beans all planted?"

"Yes, Mother," they answered. Byron remembered the feeling of guilt that had crept over him then as their mother praised them for the good job she thought they had done. It was much the same feeling of guilt that he now felt about the plan that James had suggested. And he vividly remembered how his sin had been discovered.

Ten days after the beans were planted he and his older brother went back to work in the same cornfield. The corn had grown rapidly since he last saw it, and the beans were up and growing nicely. The two brothers worked back and forth through the field, one cultivating the soil and the other loosening it up about the roots of the corn with the hoe. Then his brother suddenly remarked, "Byron, you must have planted this row twice, for there are two beans coming in every hill."

Byron noticed his brother's quizzical look and did not know what to answer. It had never occurred to him that the beans would be a telltale for his disobedient actions. It was all too true. There were the beans, side by side in plain sight, and the next row was the same. His brother at once began an inspection of the field and soon found that not only two beans but four and five had been planted in a place. Coming to the stump where the children had emptied their pails, he found beans sprouting all around.

"What does this mean, Byron?" his brother asked as he stopped and looked earnestly into Byron's face. "How did you children plant those beans?"

There was no other way than to tell the truth, and with burning cheeks he confessed his disobedience to his brother and later to his mother. She said that such deception and disobedience must be punished. Later, after the two guilty children had gone to bed, the mother quietly went to them and taught them about the harmfulness of deception and evils that were sure to follow deceit.

"Evil deeds," she said, "will sooner or later bear a harvest of bad things. You may think, Byron, that you can commit sin without having it known, but this is not true. Whenever sin is planted in the heart, it, like the beans, will surely sprout and grow."

All this ran through Byron's mind as he sat among the other boys in the woods. At last he said, "Boys, if that wouldn't be stealing, I don't know what would, and I never want to be a thief. Mother has always been downright against stealing. She has told me that a person cannot enjoy what they get dishonestly, and what I get I want to come by in an upright manner. She said, too, that a person who steals will sooner or later land behind prison bars. I could never consent to do such a thing as you have mentioned. Just think what it would mean if it would be found out!"

"Listen to that boy again!" said James, with a sneer. "He is always afraid of being found out and is forever preaching to us about what his mother has told him. I think Byron would make a pretty good preacher. He is too chicken-hearted to make his way through the world with us. What he needs is more backbone, so that he will not be afraid of doing such little things as that." Then turning to Byron he said, "It's only holding up for your rights, Byron; you are entitled to the eggs, and we will stand back of you. If any trouble ever comes, we are your right-hand men."

When James had finished his argument, the plan did not seem so bad to Byron as at the first, but he could not give his consent to carry out the suggestion even when George urged him to do so.

The shadows in the west had lengthened, and it was time that Byron was making his way homeward, so her left the boys with a hasty goodbye. Their urging remarks to consider the plan still rang in his ears as he entered the gate at home, and he feared to meet the other members of the family, lest they should read the guilt and shame that he already felt within his heart. He wondered what would happen if he did as James had suggested.

Chapter III
Misty Weather

To every youth there comes a time of conscious awakening, a time when he begins to realize that he has a part in life of his own to perform. In other words, he finds that he has an inner life that is seeking to assert itself to help him reason and decide matters that he has hitherto left or submitted to the knowledge and understanding of others.

Even the lowest and most uncultured have this Heaven-given element within them, and day by day this reasoning power increases in strength and understanding. During the time when this silent mystic power is developing within the immature mind, much mischief results from a lack of understanding of the first principles of life.

The child nestling under the protection of its parents' care little knows what dangers are ahead of it. Like the brood of chickens beneath the mother's wings, it has no comprehension of evil; and, like them, it feels the dangers when it ventures from its protection.

Byron was a child no longer. Within him the manly powers had arisen and were asserting themselves in his nature. Although unable to comprehend the full meaning of the change, he felt that he must have a right to judge and reason for himself. The current of events was sweeping him rapidly onward, and a dense mist had arisen above the sea. His course was becoming more indistinct every moment. And, both because he did not know about the hidden dangers of the deep, and also being unwilling to obey the warnings of his conscience, he was already in a perilous condition.

When Byron went to the field the next day, his mind was not on his work. He was thinking of the things that happened the day before, of James' suggestion, and of his mother's warnings. It was no light thing to act directly against his former teaching and do the very sins against which he had been warned. He was still pondering over James' plan when he returned to the barn at the noon hour.

Leaving the horses to find their own stalls, he continued to the main part of the barn. Just as he was preparing to fill one of the mangers with hay, a large white hen suddenly flew from beneath the feed box. He dropped his load quickly at the opposite side of the manger, and looked for a nest. Sure enough, it was there, and he saw that it contained three white eggs.

The suggestion arose before him that here was his opportunity. But with it came a feeling of repulsion; the thought of stealing the eggs made him shudder. But then he thought about the boys, and of the taunting remarks they would make if he came with little or no money next time. Byron hesitated. It was hard to be ridiculed and termed a coward; so he glanced about him, and then walked to the door to make sure nobody was near.

Seeing no one, he returned to the manger. But he was still fearful lest someone might be in another part of the barn, so he carefully looked all around. Still finding no one, he again stopped in front of the manger, and as he silently looked down upon the eggs he asked himself, "Shall I do it?" In answer his newly awakened manhood asserted itself, and he mumbled, "It's my right; and if I associate with those boys, there is no other way." After chiding himself for his lack of courage, he suddenly put his hand down into the nest. But just as quickly he withdrew it without taking any. The eggs were still warm, and they seemed to burn him.

Ashamed of his failure, he made another attempt. This time he succeeded in grasping the eggs firmly in his hand. With them he climbed a ladder and soon had them carefully deposited beneath a pile of hay in one corner of the loft. By this time his conscience, fully aroused, was speaking in almost audible tones, and as he got ready to enter the house, he shrank from meeting his mother. The sin that he had committed was no light thing. Not only had it broken the harmony between them, but a wall seemed to have suddenly risen. Like the beans, it was something to sprout and grow in his heart.

"Think of the days that your patient mother has spent in looking after your wants and needs. Think of the weary hours at night that she has spent beside your cradle and bedside," his conscience urged. "Can you ever heal the wounds that you are making in her heart and life? Can you ever again return her tender, loving gaze? Think of her advice concerning James. Is not his influence just as she said it would be?" The apple story and other things awoke in his memory, and when he entered the house he endeavored to slip into his accustomed place unnoticed.

Thinking that he had succeeded in his purpose, he glanced around quickly in the direction of his mother, only to see that he was mistaken. She was looking at him, and in her eyes he seemed to read the dreaded question. During the entire meal he felt that her gaze was upon him and that she was reading the hidden secrets of his heart.

Conscience suggested that he replace the stolen eggs when he returned to the barn, but the thought of the boys' ridicule and unkind remarks forced the idea from his mind. When the dinner hour was over, he returned to his work in the field, and endeavored to drown his feelings in the sea of forgetfulness and to bury his burden beneath the furrows that he was turning in the mellow soil. It helped some, for hard work often brings relief to the troubled mind. But it did not lessen his guilt nor remove the mist that had enveloped his soul and that was endangering his character and principles.

When he saw the hen fly from the manger the following day, he did not hear the warnings of his conscience quite as loudly as before. This time the eggs did not seem to burn him as he removed them from the secluded nest. Neither was he so much afraid of the eyes that might be watching him at the dinner table. Each day that week he took eggs from the manger to put with those in the loft above. He also discovered other nests in out-of-the-way places, and the eggs from them helped to increase his hidden store. Little by little the plan that had so horrified him at first came to seem entirely proper. Whenever his conscience appealed to him, he pled his rightful ownership of a share of the farm produce.

When he was able to count six dozen of the stolen eggs, he felt that they must soon be disposed of, for they might be discovered at any time. He began to wonder how to sell them. There was no place near his home to market them, and he would be missed if he left the farm for awhile. He couldn't sell them to a neighbor lest they become suspicious, and his secret be found out.

One morning as he was watering the horses at the well, and planning his work for the day, his mother came by. "Byron," she said, "we are needing flour, and it will be necessary for you to go to the mill this morning."

"Here is my chance," he thought with pleasure. "I can take the eggs with me and sell them at the country store I shall have to pass on the way. Nothing can possibly be discovered if I leave them there." Thinking it best to hide his eagerness, however, he answered carelessly, "All right. How soon shall I go? Right away?"

"Yes, you had better start at once," his mother replied. "I need the flour now and must have it as soon as I can get it." Then as she turned to go into the house she added, "Your brother will help you to prepare the load and to get started."

"Ah!" Byron remarked to himself. "I could not have wished for better luck!" As he nervously began his preparations for leaving, he wondered how he could bring the eggs down from their hiding place and get away safely with them. His older brother helped with the sacking and loading of the grain; but when the load was ready, Byron went into the barn alone to harness the horses. Before he finished, he hastily took a basket and, climbing to the loft, was soon bending over the pretty eggs. A few minutes later he had returned with them, placed the basket in a convenient place near the door, and covered it with empty grain sacks. Then he quickly returned to the horses.

When at last everything was ready, he managed, while his brother was gone, to slip the basket in among the sacks of grain. As he was driving through the gate, he smiled at the thought of his cleverness. He was pleased to think that he had escaped detection, but with this pleasure there came a bitterness and shame. What had he done? He, a thief and a robber, had stolen from his own mother. Crime was at his door! These thoughts and many more surged through his brain. Although he endeavored to excuse himself, he knew that the accusations of his conscience were true. "I can't say I have not done wrong," he at last acknowledged to himself, "but I can't back down now. I must sell these eggs, for how could I account for them if I should try to return them."

On reaching the store he stopped in front of it and, after hitching his team, lifted the basket from its hiding place. Again he was reminded of his sin, but he hesitated for only a moment.

The store had once been a home; but, having been somewhat remodeled and rearranged, it made a very respectable store building. Signs and various advertisements decorated the darkened storefront, and the many boxes and barrels in the yard signified a good amount of business.

Before entering the building, Byron stopped to examine some of the posters and found that most of them were advertising tobacco and cigars of various brands. He noticed several boxes arranged near the door, and remembered his mother telling him of loafers who often gathered about the doors of a country store to while away the time in playing cards and gambling. Instantly a scene seemed to arise before him, and in his imagination he saw a group of four men seated around one of the boxes with a deck of cards before them. The faces of the players were hard and vicious, and each man seemed intent upon winning the game and obtaining the pile of money that lay upon one corner of the box. As he gazed upon the imaginary scene, it appeared to change. The box became the green grass in the woods by the river, and the players the four young men who had played for the nickels. The same lines of sin seemed to be chiseled upon their faces, and Byron shrank from the scene.

Pushing open the screen door, he entered the store. As he met the kindly-faced grocer, he was strongly impressed with his gentlemanly appearance. After replying to the man's remarks about the weather, Byron briefly told his errand, and the grocer carried the stolen eggs away from Byron's possession, but not from his thoughts.

With his conscience still rebuking him, he began to look about the room that was a general store and post office combined. He first noticed the extreme order and neatness of the place. And then came the desire that he had long felt to own a store for himself someday. In all his dreams of the future he had pictured himself either behind a counter or in an office chair. But such a possibility seemed very far away when he thought of all the work that occupied his time upon the farm. Of late, however, his thoughts had been wholly centered upon other things.

The return of his former hopes brought again the remorse of his wrong doing, and his conscience whispered, "It would be better to recover the eggs than to blight your whole future career." But Byron simply received the change from the grocer, and when asked if there was anything else that could be done for him, he replied, "Why, yes, I will take a little candy."

He received the candy, made a few remarks about the weather and crops, and soon was again seated in the wagon. His thoughts were peculiar indeed. Byron wanted to do right. He desired not only to become a respectable citizen of his country, but to be an honor to his family as well. He meant to have a worthy aim in life. But he had not chosen the course that would land him on the shores of Success, and he knew it. He would have liked to undo the happenings of the past weeks and to begin his life anew, but thought, "It would be too hard now."

The candy purchased with the egg money he did not enjoy. It seemed to have a strange, unnatural taste, and he remembered his mother's statement that stolen goods give little enjoyment. The sight of the mill, however, changed his thoughts to other things. The building bore the signs and stains of old age, but from within came the sound of music peculiarly sweet in itself.

As the hum of the busy wheels floated out upon the morning air, it seemed to carry with it the spirit of the place. Byron remembered how pleasant the miller had been on former occasions and how interesting had been the stories that he told him while they waited for the grist to be ground into flour. He wondered if he should hear any on that particular morning and what it would be about.

Mechanically driving up to the high porch at the side of the mill, he began to unload his grain. As he did so, he heard the merry laughter of the miller as it rang out above the hum of the machinery from time to time. "He surely is happier than I am this morning," Byron thought.

Just as he unloaded the last sack of grain to place it beside the others, the miller, clad in his flour-dusted clothing, appeared in the doorway. Looking up into the happy face before him, Byron wondered if the miller ever had disappointments and trials.

"Well, Byron, I am very glad to see you here again," the miller remarked with a smile of welcome as he warmly shook the hand that had been offered him. "Everyone is well out your way, I suppose?"

Byron said they were, and asked about the grain.

"I will do the very best I can for you, Byron," the miller said kindly, "but I've had a lot of bad luck of late. Last week it was my hogs. Several of them died, and I lost quite a bit of time on account of it. And this morning, just as we were starting up, some of the machinery broke. We have it all repaired now, though, and will begin on your grist right away, as I think you are in more of a hurry than the rest of my customers. I suppose the break was caused by a small fire that we had here last week, and I'm very glad that no greater damage was done than there was."

Here his merry laughter rang out again through the building and drove away whatever dark shadows might have come at the remembrance of his troubles. Byron could see traces of the fire that had suddenly swept through the building. Even though it had been extinguished before it did very much harm, he realized the delay and damage that it must have caused the miller. Yet it had made no difference in his attitude toward others. He was just as kind and considerate as he had always been on other occasions and was as ready with his story telling. So Byron seated himself upon a pile of empty grain sacks and listened attentively.

While the miller ground the wheat, he told a story that he'd read in a certain book. It was about a young miller who had inherited his father's business. This miller made the flour for all the people in his village and for the farmers of the country for miles around. He took his pay in a toll from the grain that he ground, at the rate of one-tenth of every bushel. This tenth was measured out in a round box, or dish, that was called the toll-dish and that was kept for that special purpose.

Among this young miller's customers was an old farmer. As this man had his farm all paid for and well stocked, and having some investments besides, his neighbors considered him a rich man. He used to come about every two week to the mill, bringing four or five bags of wheat to be ground.

One day, after the old man had left, the young miller began as usual to pour the wheat into the hopper. Then a thought occurred to the miller that if he should take a little more than a tenth the farmer would never miss it. "Other millers do it," said he to himself, "and so might I as well. Besides, I will make it up to him by extra care in grinding his flour."

So, after he had taken out the tenth that he was entitled to, he filled the toll-dish twice again and poured it into a barrel of his own wheat that stood near.

But the miller did not feel altogether satisfied with what he had done. The thought of it disquieted him more than once. Yet he could not quite persuade himself to put the wheat back. "I think I'm fairly entitled to something more from such a rich man," he reasoned.

Then a bright thought struck him. There was in the mill some corn that belonged to a widow. The poor woman had brought it there in a wheelbarrow herself, and left it to be ground into meal.

"I'll take less than my full share from her, and so will make matters square by remembering the poor."

This seemed for a time to satisfy his conscience. But, having made a beginning, he gradually increased the amount he took from the rich farmer, but soon stopped giving any extra to the widow.

The young miller had guessed right that the farmer wouldn't miss what he'd taken. But he was wrong in thinking that he could keep his conscience quiet. He found that it would not heal while he kept on wounding it afresh, or that it would accept as true what he knew to be false. It was of the kind that we find it so inconvenient to have when we want to do wrong and still be as comfortable as if we were doing right.

"Why has he chosen this particular story this morning?" thought Byron, as he changed his position upon the grain sacks. Byron would have liked something of a different nature much better, but he continued to listen respectfully as the miller went on talking.

The young miller of the story was in the habit of going to the village church on a Sunday. Here he sat in the pew with his wife and little children, taking part in the service and listening to the minister's sermon. But now, whenever the eighth commandment was mentioned, he grew restless and uneasy and anxious for the service to be over.

On weekdays the stage driver, as he passed the mill door, threw out a newspaper that the miller subscribed to. And as the great waterwheel was revolving and the millstones were grinding, it had been his favorite pastime to sit among the bags of grain in his flour-besprinkled clothes and read his paper through and through. But of late he found himself avoiding all paragraphs headed: "Theft," "Embezzlement," "Breach of Trust," "Fraud." Now and then he happened on an account of some honest debtor who as soon as he was able paid up his back debts, or of some repentant thief who made restitution for the things he had stolen. This was unpleasant reading to the miller.

In the village there lived a man who had not paid his debts, and in consequence bore a bad name. The miller disliked meeting this man. And occasionally the miller, while on business to the county seat, passed by the jail. Peering through the bars, he often saw the evil countenances of the prisoners. "What are they in there for, I wonder," he said to himself. "The truth is, I deserve to be there with them."

And so the miller found a rebuke in whatever he came across. This went on until everything about him seemed to join in a dreadful chorus, accusing him of his crime.

At last the load on his conscience became so heavy that he could bear it no longer. But what should he do to get rid of it? To confess his guilt would crush him to the earth. There was but one thing more dreadful, and that was to go on hiding it. But was there no way of escaping an open confession? Ah! happy thought! This would not be necessary. The farmer was still confidently bringing his grain every two weeks to the mill.

"I will go over my accounts," said the miller to himself, "and add up to the last pound all I have ever taken from him. I will return it gradually with his flour, from time to time, in quantities that will not be noticed. Thus I shall pay my debt and clear my conscience without being even suspected of wrong."

Having made this resolve, he longed to put it in practice, and could hardly wait for the farmer's next trip. In a few days he arrived as usual. The miller, with a glad heart (which he was careful to conceal), carried the bags into the mill and bade the farmer a cheerful "goodbye" as he drove away.

"Now," he thought, "I will take out of this grinding some of my toll. For if I don't take any out, the difference might be noticed." So he filled the toll-dish three times instead of six, and ground up the rest of the wheat.

But while he was secretly carrying out his plan at the mill, he little suspected how matters stood at the farmhouse. The farmer's wife, who had occasion to notice the wheat more than her husband, had suspected for some time that the flour returned from the mill seemed short in weight. At last she told her husband.

"Nonsense!" he said. "I've known the miller all his life, and his father before him: his father had a conscience, and so has he."

At this Byron glanced quickly out the window and thought of his own conscience. But his companion went on with his story.

"Well," said the farmer's wife, "there's one way of testing it to make certain. I weighed what we last sent him; now we'll weigh what he sends back to us."

So the farmer agreed to this. The next day he went to the mill for the grinding. The miller received him gladly and hastened to carry out the grist to the wagon. As he drove homeward the farmer said to himself, "How strange that Wife should speak so about the flour! But women do sometimes take up such queer notions. She'll be waiting when I get home, I'm sure, to have the bags put on the scales as soon as they are unloaded."

He was not wrong. As he drove around to the side porch, his wife appeared in her great white apron, hardly able to keep quiet until the wagon was backed up. As the bags were taken down, they were laid, one by one, on the scales that stood near.

"How does it come out, Wife?" asked the farmer as she wrote down the pounds contained in the last bag.

But she kept on going over the figures again and again without answering; so the old man put on his spectacles and hastily added them up.

"Didn't I tell you so?" he exclaimed both reproachfully and

triumphantly. "Why, instead of cheating us, he has cheated himself! What a pity it is for a woman to be suspicious!"

"Don't brag too soon," said his wife, annoyed. "You'd better wait till we've weighed another grinding."

The hungry mouths on the farm soon demanded a fresh supply of flour, and then another load of wheat was weighed with extra care and hauled to the mill.

The miller, with some relief to his conscience by the little he had already done, was more eager than ever to carry out his plan and remove his burden altogether. "It is certain they have not noticed anything unusual in the last grist," he thought. "I might just as well hurry matters up a little. This time I'll take out no toll at all, and after this will begin adding some of my own flour."

Putting off other farmers who had brought their grain first, the miller ground the old man's wheat before theirs and sent him word it was ready. The farmer's wife, still smarting under the charge of being unjustly suspicious, hurried him away after it, and waited his return even more anxiously than she had when he was bringing the former load. It came in due time, and was promptly laid on the scales as the other had been. But if she was surprised before, she was dumb with wonder now. Her husband, who, in truth, thought there was no better woman, seeing her embarrassment, was considerate enough not to chide her. So the flour was quietly put away in the storeroom.

Just before bedtime that evening, as they sat together in their old-fashioned comfortable kitchen, the farmer said to his wife, "I've been thinking about that last grist. There must be something the matter with our young miller's scales, and you know that we don't want to take what belongs to him without paying for it. I mean to go over to the mill tomorrow on purpose to look into it."

"That's exactly what I want you to do," replied his wife, seriously. "The grinding was short of weight more than once, I know; and twice now it has weighed too much, we both know. The thing keeps worrying my mind."

As soon as breakfast was over the next morning, the farmer harnessed up his horses and drove to the mill. The miller, standing at the door, was surprised to see him, since he had neither wheat to grind nor flour to haul away. Then a look of apprehension came over his face, for there is always a lurking fear of evil in the heart that is conscious of hiding some wrong.

"I don't believe you can guess what I've come over about," said the farmer, as he got down from the wagon.

The miller said nothing.

"Did you weigh the last grinding?" asked the old man.

"Yes."

"And the one before that?"

"Yes."

"And don't you know they weighed too much? But perhaps you wanted to make us a present!" he continued, merrily. "Or maybe, as winter is coming on, you thought we stood in need."

The miller's face grew scarlet. He attempted to speak, but his voice stuck in his throat, and he could not utter a word.

The farmer saw at a glance that the miller was in trouble, and said kindly, "Tell me all about it. I was your father's friend and am yours."

Then the miller took the old man into the mill, and, shutting the door, told him, in a trembling voice, the whole sad story.

"I've found out," he said, "that the wrong way is a hard way. I'm in that way yet, but I long to get out of it. I'd give this mill—yes, and all that is in it—were that needful to make me feel myself once more an honest man. I have set it all aside. Those bags of wheat over there contain every pound I have ever taken. But I shall never know a happy moment till I see them hauled away from here and put into your barn."

"My dear young friend," said the farmer, drawing his sleeve across his eyes, "I care nothing for the flour, yet it is mine, and it is right I should take it. Carry it out and load it on the wagon and I'll soon put it where you want it to be. I believe you have been taught, by the best of teachers, such a lesson as you'll never forget. And be assured that after this, I shall never fear to trust you. Take my word for it, too, that no one but my wife—and she can keep a secret—shall ever hear of this."

The next Sunday the miller went to church, and, whatever else he might have dreaded to hear about, it was not the eighth commandment. And the following week, and for many a week afterward, he read his newspaper as he did in former time—all through, skipping nothing.

After finishing the story the miller added a few words on principle. "Principle," he told Byron, "is that quality within man that makes him do right because it is right. It acts as a rudder and helps him to take and keep the right course all through life's voyage. It guides him during the storms of temptation. His companions may be willing to slight their work, but he will be independent and will judge his duty to others by what he would expect from them.

"This young miller's sufferings were the result of his acting against his principles and failing to heed the warnings of his conscience. Byron, men or boys without principle may sometimes succeed in business; but, mark my word, if they do, not only will they reap unhappiness all the way along, but, in the end, sorrow and misery will be their reward. I had rather act according to my principle—to do right and listen to the warnings of my conscience—than to have all the wealth that is gained by dishonesty."

Here the miller was called to another part of the building, and Byron was left alone for awhile. His heart was beating wildly. Shame and guilt had done their work, and he wondered, "Would it be possible to undo the happenings of the past few weeks?" He realized more keenly than ever what dishonesty really means, and his sin seemed to loom up before him mountain high.

He could hear the miller's merry whistle now and then, and noted the pleasant smile with which he greeted his workmen and customers. And Byron thought, "It must surely be principle that has given his face that happy, care-free expression."

A picture of the two great courses in life arose before Byron. He saw that he had chosen the wrong course, and he partly discerned the mist that had so thickly enveloped him. The dense fog was breaking away; but as it did so, dangers great and forbidding appeared. The course the miller in the story had taken in the end was not tempting, but Byron saw that it was right.

At last his flour was ready, and he started home. As he rode along, he meditated on the story. It revealed to him his own duty, and his conscience strove to guide him aright by proposing plans of reconciliation between him and his mother.

"It would be better to tell her at once," whispered that faithful voice in his ear. "Explain the temptation and sin that have befallen you, and allow her to advise you. She will be only too glad to help you out of your difficulties."

"Yes, but the boys," he reasoned. "How can I meet their taunts when I see them?"

"Don't see them! Stay out of their company, and you will have no trouble," his conscience continued.

"How about Sunday? I shall have to see them at Sunday school, and hard questions will be asked!" Byron argued.

"You could avoid the boys," conscience suggested. "Just let them understand that you do not want their company."

"Which is easier said than done," thought Byron, as he drove in through the gateway at his home.

Chapter IV
In the Tide

An hour may seem to be prolonged to a year in the mind where there is suspense. Thus the day had crept by for Byron's mother. She realized that the strong unity which had existed between her and her son was broken. The thought that he no longer confided in her as in the past pierced and stung her heart as a poisoned dagger would have done. Though the duties of the day were pressing, she thought continually of her son. "Why are we drifting so far apart? How can I get him to tell the secret that has become a barrier between us?" she pondered. "If only I could get a clue that would enable me to draw from him the secret that is separating us, how gladly I would grasp it!"

She heard Byron driving into the yard and appeared in the doorway to greet him with a smile; but his eyes were turned away from the house, and although she called he did not appear to hear. Returning to the stove where she was preparing the meal, she continued her meditation. It was not until late in the evening that she found herself alone with her son.

For a time after his return from the mill, Byron struggled with the conviction that he should keep his secret from his mother no longer. But he did not obey the first impulses to go to her, so his decision was weakened and to tell her seemed harder than ever. Little by little excuses for himself and the boys arose in his mind, and as he considered them he felt relief and decided to wait at least until the following morning. He was just preparing to steal away unnoticed to his bedroom when his mother met him and requested him to take the chair that she offered him.

With an earnest prayer in her heart, his mother endeavored to draw from her son the cause of his changed attitude toward her, but in vain. He listened to her tender, loving words as one in a dream, making no response. As she finished her talk and bade him goodnight, she kissed him tenderly and whispered, "Byron dear, is something troubling you? You can surely tell me about it, can you not? I might be able to help you out of your difficulty if I knew. Open up your heart and tell me all." But Byron simply shook his head and hastened away into his own room.

Long into the night he continued to think of his mother's kindness and love, and how she had explained the sorrow and misery that come to many people simply because they continually refuse to accept instruction and advice. But as a drowsiness crept over him, the cruel remarks of the boys and his fear of their displeasure were uppermost in his mind. There had already been too many failures, he reasoned, and good resolutions must be a thing of the past.

There once was a ship about to make a voyage. The time of starting had arrived; the farewells by the passengers had been said; the gangway that connected them with the land had been withdrawn; and the boat was being rocked from side to side by its efforts to launch out into the deep. But although the machinery was in motion, no headway was being made. At last the cause was discovered. One of the cables, which had not been unfastened, was holding them to the pier. As soon as the line was untied, the ship began speeding away from the shallow water.

It was much the same with Byron. He was being held by his fear of the boys, but the taste of the pleasure of sin made it difficult for him to break away from their company. His conscience was pointing out the trouble to him, but he was not heeding advice. Instead, he was wasting precious moments and was dreaming of the fairyland of pleasure that he had been told was upon the land, and longing to view it for himself. He was where the tide of the world could play with him at will, where it could lash and beat him about at every turn.

Morning dawned bright and clear, and little birds sang merry songs as they had so often done before. But it was not until the sunlight stole across the room to his pillow and shone on his face that Byron awoke. His mother downstairs was preparing the breakfast, and he could hear the rattle of the dishes as she placed them upon the table.

"I didn't dream it was so late," he remarked to himself, as he sprang from the bed and began to dress. "I wonder if Mother has forgotten to call me."

He had been called some time before, but his mother only smiled and bade him good morning as he passed her on his way to the barn. She had always been gentle with her children, and Byron had not gone so deeply into sin that he was wholly unmindful of this.

Her earnest words of the previous evening returned to his mind as he went about his morning duties.

"My son," she had said, "The world is full of sin and wickedness, but it is not the things that God has created that are causing this shame. It's the wrong use of them. Take for example, the delicious fruit of the vineyard and the different grains that are grown in the field. See the ungodly uses these products are put to when they are made into wines and liquors. And again, look at these wines and liquors upon the shelves of the saloon. They could not harm man if he would let them alone. It is the wrong use of them that caused all the trouble they produce.

"Carefully examine the tobacco plant and you'll find it perfectly harmless in itself and to the worms that feed upon it. It wasn't intended to share a place among our foods. Man has made a wrong use of it.

"The beautiful poppy is not to blame for the millions who are lulled to sleep through the use of opium. Man is responsible for all the harm caused by opium and drugs like it. He has put the articles manufactured from these natural products to a dishonorable use.

"Man was made in God's own image, just a little lower than the angels. He fell from this holy plane through Satan's efforts, and now, by Satan's help and suggestions, he abuses and misuses the things that would otherwise be a blessing to all humanity.

"It is sad that this is so, but since it is, we don't need to obey Satan and follow his example. You will no doubt sometime be tempted to partake of liquor, tobacco, and perhaps opium; but it lies within your power to resist the temptation. All of these powerful articles have similar effects upon the system, according to their strength. They all produce addictions and cravings, dull the senses, and bind with habits from which few are able to escape."

The words of Byron's mother returned to him as tiny darts. As he pondered them, they seemed to vibrate in the air about him. When he passed the manger, he did not look beneath the feed trough for eggs. Once more he felt that he would like to unburden his heart to his mother; but when he returned to the house, he ate his breakfast in silence and afterward hurried away to the field.

The day passed as many others had done before it, and at last he went once more to visit his cousin, with the permission of his mother to spend the night with him. He carried, hidden in his pocket, the money that he had received for the stolen eggs.

As soon as it was possible for the cousins to do so they quietly slipped away down by the riverside, and it was not long until they were joined by the other boys. James and George had been anxiously waiting for Byron's appearance. They were not quite sure whether he would actually try, or succeed in carrying out, the plan that they had suggested for getting more money. They were therefore ready with questions about it as soon as he arrived.

Now it was that Byron could open his heart, but it was in a much different way from that in which he had resolved to tell his mother. He told them about hiding and selling the eggs. When he had finished, the boys patted him upon the back and called him a good fellow, and they told him that he was making rapid progress and would someday be up with them.

"And now, boys," James continued, "I have our program for this evening all arranged. There's to be a dance at a public hall two miles away from here, and I thought we'd all enjoy attending. I've never danced very much myself, but I want to learn more about it. And here is Byron it is high time he was being initiated!"

Byron's heart began beating fast. He endeavored to be calm, but in spite of his efforts his mother's face and warnings again came before him. He had heard about those dances at the hall ever since his earliest recollection, and he knew that only a low class of people made up the crowds. He had been taught that dancing was one of the great evils that led on to the baser things of life. He had never attended one of these gatherings, and he had no desire to do so. But he was already in the tide, and such things might be expected frequently.

"Now, see here, boys," he said, "you are constantly springing something new upon me whenever we meet of late. Where is this thing going to end?" He wanted to tell them some of the things that his mother had told him about dancing, but he realized that he would only be laughed at.

"Why, of course we want something new," George said. "Do you suppose we always want to go along in the same old way? We want to keep apace with the times. Why, a fellow might as well be dead as to be behind the times! Oh, Byron, come along and get rid of that idea of yours about not wanting to learn new things!"

"Yes, but there's something more to it than that," Byron answered. "We can't go to that dance without having people see us. Those with whom I'm acquainted know very well that my mother doesn't approve of my going to such places, and the thing will be sure to be found out. If once it's found out, there'll be an investigation started that will deprive us of each other's company hereafter."

"Oh, Byron, you're always afraid something awful is going to happen," answered James. "It's the same old story every time. You know very well that everything has been running smoothly and that all has been kept a secret. There'll be no one at that dance that will run to your mother with the news. They'll be only too glad to see you there, and will be your friends; they and won't tell on you."

After a little more persuasion the boys started on their way, and they soon arrived at the hall. The dance had already begun. The music was grand, and the dancers kept perfect time and answered every call. It was all new to Byron, and he could not help enjoying the scene.

Suddenly as he sat watching, someone tapped him on the shoulder and said, "What are you doing here? I thought your mother didn't believe in your attending such places." The speaker was a neighbor boy that lived only a short distance from Byron's home. Byron hardly knew what to answer him, but said that he had come there with some friends. As soon as it was possible, he got out of the boy's presence.

In every part of the room Byron ran across those whom he knew, and thus the evening was spoiled for him. After he had passed an hour in trying to dodge acquaintances, his companions bade him come with them to the farther end of the hall, where soft drinks and other things were kept for sale.

"We might as well get the benefit of our egg money," James said with a very important air as he ordered a number of things and told Byron to pay for them. The last purchase made was that of some cigars.

Now, Byron had never smoked, but he remembered distinctly an experience he had with tobacco the winter before. His mother had gotten some tobacco leaves from a neighbor to be used in some way among the poultry, and Byron had thought, since he had never tasted tobacco, that he should like to see just what it was like. The opportunity to try it came one evening while he was on his way to feed the pigs. The dried leaves were hanging in the granary, and after securing his corn for the pigs, he pinched a piece from a wide brown leaf and began to chew it. It did not taste at all as he had expected it would, and he could not understand why anyone would want to chew such nasty-tasting stuff.

But he continued chewing it all the way to the pigpen, which was quite a distance from the granary. He was already beginning to feel faint when he set down his basket, and by the time he had finished throwing the corn to the pigs, he was so faint and dizzy that he could not stand up. He somehow managed to get out of sight behind the pen, and there he sat down. It was several minutes before the spell had passed off.

As Byron took the cigar, he also remembered a talk his teacher made to the school the previous winter, in which she explained the effects upon the human system of the poisons contained in whiskey and tobacco. Also, a story that he had read in a book flashed across his mind—the story of a lion and a tiger that did much harm in a certain village. Both of these animals were fierce and savage. They roamed about the village during many hours of the night and sometimes during the day, and often killed some of the people. In fact, the animals had such power that at every public gathering several people were killed. For some reason the people thought that the beasts must be allowed to live, as it would not be wise to kill them. They were really handsome creatures and able to attract so much attention that it was decided best to chain them in a certain part of the city where they could be seen by the people as they passed along the streets. Accordingly they were both chained and great signs and advertisements were scattered abroad urging the people to become interested in the animals.

When the people heard that the beasts, which had before been such a terror to them, were chained, they rushed in such masses to see them that, notwithstanding the chains, many in various ways fell an easy prey to the deadly claws. Then, too, some young men, thinking that it would be manly and smart to tease the ferocious beasts, fell beneath their mighty paws. Even the fathers and mothers sometimes became the prey. At last such an agonizing cry had risen from the hearts of the people that some of the citizens became aroused and declared that the animals ought to be killed. This they soon found was no easy matter, for the most of the people said, "Let them live." And the men and women who urged their destruction were declared insane. So the animals were allowed to live on and continued their deadly work of death among the inhabitants of the village.

The lion and tiger that did so much harm among the people, Byron remembered, were whiskey and tobacco, and they would continue to cause destruction and misery just as long as they were manufactured and placed in the reach of the people. His conscience warned him now of his danger, and he knew better than to have anything to do with the poisonous stuff. But he saw the other boys lighting their cigars, and he thought, "I don't believe smoking tobacco would be as bad as chewing the leaves." So, after getting a match, he began another new experience.

He used several matches before he succeeded in lighting the cigar, but finally he was puffing tiny clouds of smoke into the air just as his companions were doing. All seemed well for a time, but suddenly a feeling of sickness stole over him, and he told the boys that he would have to go outside, where he could breathe the fresh air.

James, with a laugh, told him that smoking always did that to people at first, and assured him that he would soon be all right. But Byron did not want to finish his cigar even after he was in the fresh air and was feeling better. He even thought that he would never want to smoke again.

The evening had not been pleasant for him. The old proverb, "A guilty conscience needs no accusing," was too true in his case. He had tried to enjoy the music but it was spoiled through his fear that he would be noticed, and he had not enjoyed the things that he had purchased with the egg money at all.

After leaving the dance hall, the boys soon separated. As Byron walked along with his cousin, he thought of his mother's words about things that were gotten dishonestly. In all the things he had been doing of late he could find no pleasure whatever. The money for which he had schemed and risked so much was gone, and for what! He shuddered as he thought of the cigars and wished that the eggs were all back in their nests again and that he had never taken part in the plan suggested by the boys.

Several days passed before Byron was able to rid himself of his bad feelings and overcome the fearful foreboding that someone was coming to "tell on" him. But as day after day passed by and nobody came, he felt a great relief and thoughts of the cigar no longer made his head feel dizzy.

One Sunday afternoon, three weeks from the time the boys had been together before, they went to the loft of an old barn owned by the farmer for whom James worked. James' employer was not interested in the company of his hired help, so their friends were seldom brought into the farmhouse.

Upon this occasion James had a surprise planned for the boys. He waited until they were all comfortably seated upon the hay, and then in a new dignified tone he said, "Boys, I've got a new book. It's one that I believe will be of real interest to us all. I consider it very valuable and something we need to read before we go any further with our plans. We can take turns in reading it, and then no one will be especially tired."

"Oh, go on with your book!" George exclaimed roughly. "I never did like books, and I never shall. I always hated to go to school because books and I are such poor friends! They always seemed so dry to me."

"This is none of your dry kind, George," James said reassuringly. "Every page is full of good things. Why, I was so carried away with it that I hardly knew whether it was morning or evening."

"Well, James, if you have such an interesting book, we had better look it over," George said in a patronizing tone. So James hastened to his room and soon returned with a small yellow book called The Life of Jesse James.

Now, Byron had heard of the James boys and of some of their wild and daring deeds, but he had also been warned of the dangers in the future of those who read the account of their reckless lives. Of course, his conscience reproved him, but how could advice so often unheeded be of any service in times of danger now? He heard the voice that had spoken, but, oh, it was now so far away that it seemed only an echo of the past.

As the boys listened to the thrilling accounts, James' enthusiasm increased, and he said, "Boys, it takes real courage and bravery to rob a bank or a train and get away with booty."

Byron thought of his experience with the eggs as James went on to say, "It fairly makes my hair stand on end when I think of the close quarters they got into, and of how they often had to shoot their way out."

"It surely does!" Byron added with feeling. "And," he added, "I don't see what enjoyment they got out of the money they took or from the things bought with it. They never could feel free and easy while they had it, for they were continually thinking that they might be found out, and were in constant danger!"

The night at the dance hall seemed to loom up before Byron, and he seemed to hear again his mother's words on how things that are gotten dishonestly are not enjoyed.

Seeing the course of Byron's thoughts, James said emphatically, "Why, of course they had a good time! They had all the money they desired, and when that was gone they knew how to get more. I've been getting some good points from this book that will be helpful to us. We've been too backward and it's time we began to move out a little. There's no need of us fellows going through life without more money. It's for us if we will just go after it.

"The other day when I was over to the store, I sized up the situation pretty thoroughly, and I believe that some night we can get in through one of the rear windows and help ourselves to what is there. George and I have been preparing ourselves for such a raid, and we want you, Byron, to join us. Of course, this will be only a starter. But as we proceed, our courage and bravery will increase and after a while the brave deeds of which we have been reading this afternoon will not outshine us very far."

The reading of the book Byron had somewhat enjoyed; but the proposal that he take part in the robbing of a store was more than he could stand. He thought that if he should do such a thing and end up being just as guilty as he had been on account of the eggs, while hardly getting any pleasure, he did not want to have any part in this new scheme. So he said, "Boys, this thing is going too far. Just as sure as I am sitting here, if we enter into this stealing business, it will leak out some way and the prison cell will be our fate."

"There—there it is again!" George said with a sneer, as James had been in the habit of doing. "Our preacher has gotten his text ready for another sermon! Byron, you are always getting scared before there's any danger. James and I are both older than you are, and we know several things that you don't know. Now our experience has been greater than yours, and if you'll listen to a little reason and common sense you'll come along all right. This thing of the people finding out everything we do is all bosh. Most every night James and I are out together, and we're having some fine times of late, and no one has caught us yet or even suspected us. They think we're all right because we go to Sunday school on Sunday."

"Don't you fool yourself, George," Byron answered. "There's more than one who doesn't look upon you boys as angels, by any means, and among that number is my mother. Of course, she doesn't know just what you're doing, but she's afraid to have me associate with you too much."

"See here, Byron! You will have to get rid of some of your fanatical ideas about your mother. Mothers are all right in their proper place, but they have never been boys. What do they know about what a boy should do! All your mother thinks about is trying to keep you from having a good time."

Deeply stung by these words, Byron flushed. He knew that his mother was a good woman, but he could not reply without being laughed at.

"When Byron gets a little more experience, he will see things differently," James said almost kindly, a moment later. Then turning to Byron, he said, "If you could only go out a few nights with George and me, it would be a great help to you in getting rid of some of your fears. Why not break loose from the restraint you're under? Just let your mother know that you're old enough to look out for yourself. Set a date to meet us sometime and we'll have a grand old time."

"Yes, but Mother would want to know where I was going, and then there would be trouble," Byron answered.

"Let the trouble come," James replied. "It will soon blow over. You're old enough to do as you please, and there's no need of always being tied down to her. Suppose we all plan to meet here next Saturday night, and I'll try to arrange for the rest."

"Planning is fine," Byron said, "but to get here will be another thing altogether. Mother will not consent to my coming."

"I'll tell you what I would do, Byron," said George, who had been quietly listening. "I would just go to her and tell her that I would like to spend the night with James and go with him to Sunday school the next morning. If she doesn't consent, I would simply take the law in my own hands and go regardless of her wishes. It will have to come to that sooner or later, anyway, so you might as well break the ice now."

Byron promised to try to be with them upon the following Saturday night, but had little hope of success. Soon after the conversation the boys parted. The following week passed swiftly by, and the Saturday evening which begins this story soon arrived. Byron was on his way to the place where James was working.

The tide had done its work.

Chapter V
Danger Signals

As Byron paused on the foot log, the evening that this story began, his conscience endeavored to point out the danger signals that were about and ahead of him.

He felt the weight of his disobedience and sin. He thought of the many prayers his dear mother had offered for his protection, and he vividly remembered her earnest entreaties upon that particular night. Her last words, "My dear boy, I shall pray for you!" sent a thrill through his heart. "Is she praying—is she thinking of me this very moment?" he wondered. Then the hoot of the owl again rang out through the forest.

"Why not return to Mother and pour out before her my heartaches and beg her forgiveness for all of my shortcomings?" he thought. "How her tender touch upon my forehead and her loving words would soothe my troubled mind!" But again the thought of George and James returned and overcame his better judgment. "They are probably waiting for me right now," he said aloud, "and what would they say if they knew I had such thoughts! I must have more courage or I will never succeed! When I get out of these woods, I may feel differently. The stars at least will be shining, and that will be a help."

Hastening on he followed first a narrow path and then an old forest road, until he came out upon the highway. When the rustling of the leaves and the breaking of twigs beneath his feet ceased, he felt relieved, for something like fear had followed him through the woods and the prophesied dangers seemed close upon him.

In another half-hour he entered the yard that surrounded the home of the farmer for whom James worked, and the lights from the house fell softly upon the walk before him. In the shadow just beyond he stopped, for he thought that he heard voices in the dark recesses of the porch. He was not mistaken, for he soon found James and George anxiously awaiting his arrival and commenting upon his non-appearance.

"At last!" he heard them exclaim as he drew near.

"Here we have been an hour or more waiting for you and expecting you every minute!" James exclaimed. "What was the matter, Byron? Was it trouble with the old woman that kept you?"

The disrespect and unkindness of these remarks hurt Byron very much, but he dared not say anything about it, knowing they would ridicule him if he did.

"I was delayed in getting started," he said.

He did not need to say any more, because James exclaimed, "Boys, it's getting late now, and I'll have to go to the store for the mail. If you'll go with me, we can be planning something on our way. I intended to plan everything out before we came together, but so many things were suggested to my mind that I really could not decide upon any of them, so I have no plan for tonight. But we'll have plenty of time as we walk to the post office, as it is two miles away."

As the boys walked along in the darkness, James and George grew very merry and rehearsed several exciting adventures, but Byron remained silent. His experience had been quite different from theirs in every way, and the scenes of the past few hours had not all vanished. He was still thinking of the words that were spoken to him at the river.

Suddenly George said, "It seems to me as though Byron is unusually quiet tonight. I never knew him to be so still before. I wonder if he's losing his power of speech? Why don't you wake up, old fellow, and be yourself again?"

So Byron did try to become sociable, and joined in the conversation, but his thoughts were elsewhere.

Two letters and a newspaper were waiting for the farmer at the post office. James quickly thrust them into his pocket, and, stepping to the counter, he purchased some fruit, candy, and cigars for his group.

It was with reluctance that Byron took the cigar James offered him, for he still remembered his experience at the dance hall. But he was anxious to avoid the remarks of the boys, so he placed it between his lips, and when it was lighted he began to smoke. In a few minutes the three passed out into the darkness, but Byron was already feeling the effects of the tobacco upon his system. Now that the boys could not see him, he threw the cigar from him as though it had been a snake.

While passing a country church, they saw that some kind of service was being held, and their attention was attracted to a group of young men and boys who were loitering about on the outside. The coarse words and rough laughter excited their curiosity. Joining the group, they listened to several vulgar stories.

Among the faces George recognized that of his friend and neighbor Jason White. Jason was several years older than either of the boys, but George introduced him to his friends and also invited him to join them. Jason was only too glad to accept the invitation and said that he was anxious for something of the kind. The four were soon wending their way along the highway. As they were passing a certain farmhouse, George remarked, "Here is where old Davis lives. He's a stingy old codger. I'd like to get even with him. He has had it in for my dad for a long time. Last fall James and I got in his melon patch one night, and he happened to be watching. He fired us out in a hurry, but he never knew who it was. The big farm he owns here is making lots of money. He would never have missed the few melons that we could have taken."

"Perhaps he would have given you some if you had asked him for them," Byron said quickly, for he was acquainted with Mr. Davis himself and knew him to be a kind man.

"Not much! He's not made that way," George answered excitedly. "He's a regular old crank, and besides, that is not our way of getting things. Here is his orchard, and who is getting any good from that but himself?"

As they passed by the house, they all became very quiet, and, climbing the fence on the opposite side of the road, they entered a fine young orchard of apple trees. George stepped up to one of the trees and said, "I'm going to see that no one gets any good from some of these trees!" With his knife he quickly cut the bark from around six of the young trees. "That will fix them, all right," he said with a laugh of satisfaction. "I don't believe in returning good for evil."

At the lower end of the field was a vacant house that they said was some more of old Davis' possessions. Just as they were passing, crash went a window pane. In the stillness of the night the noise of the breaking glass sounded like the report of a gun. All suddenly stopped, and Byron asked, "What was that?"

James answered, "Oh, I was just helping George to get even with old Davis."

At this the other boys began to laugh, and for a few minutes clods, stones, and clubs were showered against the house until the sound of the breaking glass might have been heard for a long distance. Fearful lest someone might see or hear them, they ran across a field to another road. "Whose house is this?" George queried as they stopped in front of a fine residence.

"Oh, that is where Sibleys live," Jason said quickly. Then, suddenly calling their attention to some chickens that were roosting in a tree not far from the house, he continued in a low tone, "Say, boys, I have an idea. Let's have a chicken roast tonight. You fellows keep out of sight in the shadow of the fence, and I will see to the rest."

Crouching down, as one who understands his business, Jason started toward the house. For a few minutes there was perfect silence, and then the little group in the fence corner heard the flapping of wings, followed by a few smothered squawks. Instinctively they started to run, and they did not stop until they came to the river. Jason was not far behind them. In his hands he carried two plump chickens. The quickly crossed to the opposite bank and threw themselves panting upon the grass, commenting upon their narrow escape, for Jason had noticed several persons appearing at the window next to the tree as he left the Sibley house. Then they began to plan for the dressing, cooking, and eating of their pillage.

"This would be an excellent place to clean these fowls," Jason suggested. "I'm pretty sure I wasn't seen by anyone looking out the window, and no one would think of looking for us in this out-of-the-way spot. So we can work without any fear of danger."

James and George agreed, and the three began to do the work, but Byron sat and did nothing. He could not enjoy such proceedings.

Everything they did was new, and strangely exciting to him. But he dared not express his opinions, for the others would only reproach and ridicule him, and he knew that he had no excuse for being in their company.

He was constantly drawing closer to the danger signals and was filled with fear and awe at the sight. Only a short time before he had stood upon the foot log a little farther up this same stream and listened to the warnings of his slighted conscience.

"Poor Mother!" he thought. "Is she still awake? Did she pray for me as she said she would? Is she still praying for me? Or is she lying upon a pillow that is wet with tears?" These and many other questions were in his mind. For awhile, in the excitement of their work, the older boys quite forgot about Byron.

When the dressing of the chickens was done, Jason said, "Now, boys, we must find a place where we can cook and eat our spoil. I know of a vacant house about a half mile back from the main road. I believe that will be an ideal place to roast our chickens, and if you will all follow I will lead you safely there."

To follow their leader along the narrow path near the river was no easy matter, but with care they managed to do so. At length they reached the highway, and traveling was easier. As they sped along, Byron glanced longingly into the windows of the houses that were still lighted. He wished that he was home and safe in bed instead of trudging about the country in such a disgraceful manner. How gladly he would have crept silently up the stairway to his own bedroom, for he was very weary indeed. Instead he must follow the boys, making as little noise as possible. Now far from the Sibleys', where the chickens had been stolen, they turned suddenly down a narrow lane and soon were standing in front of a deserted house.

"This place has been vacant quite awhile," Jason said as he carefully examined the doors. Finding them all locked, he said a little disappointedly, "Where there is a will, there is a way, and I have the will to enter this house." The tone of his voice made Byron uneasy.

After Jason had tried all the windows and found them securely nailed, he seized a long fence post that was lying near, and smash went every pane of glass in the window nearest him.

"What on earth are you doing?" Byron exclaimed, rushing forward. He had been standing a little part from the rest, secretly hoping that something might turn up that would give him an excuse to return home. Perhaps he had thinking of another danger signal, and the sound of the breaking glass made him think that it was near at hand.

"I am only making a way where there is no way," Jason replied, as he quickly climbed through the opening he had made. Hastening to a door, he threw it open, saying gleefully as he did so, "Step into my parlor, boys. It's as pretty a little place as you could wish!"

When the boys had entered the musty room, and had lighted a match, they saw that it was empty, except for some old rubbish that had been left by the family who had formerly occupied it. In one corner there was an old fireplace.

"Good!" Jason said as his eyes fell upon the uninviting hearth; "this is just what we want! Now, while I light another match, you fellows hustle about and bring material for a fire."

Obeying the command of Jason, the boys soon had a good fire built from the rubbish that was strewn about the room. As the flames began to leap and roar up the chimney, the four could see better what they were doing.

George suddenly exclaimed, "Get something up to those windows as quickly as you can. The light of this fire can be easily seen from the road. Get newspapers, or anything, but hurry!" An armful of newspapers were brought from an adjoining room, and the light from the fire was soon shut away from public view.

So exciting had been the proceedings that again Byron was forgotten. When he was again noticed, it was by James, who said, "Why, Byron, what is the matter with you? You look as though you had seen a ghost."

He had, for the ghost of his former self had been continually before him, and he was heartsick and troubled. The entire evening had indeed been a trying time for Byron, but the excitement of the past hour had quite upset him. He stood there in the firelight, weak and faint, like a shadow of his former self.

The boys waited, and at last he said, "Boys, there is certainly no fun in this for me. I would rather be at home in bed. I don't believe in omens, but I fear that this night's doing are going to end up bad. I have had a strange experience since I left home, and my feelings are indescribable."

"That's nothing new," James said mockingly. "Byron is subject to this kind of spells. This is not the first one that he has had by any means. The pace that we have been going tonight is just a little fast for him, and he is always ready to get scared at his own shadow. Still he is not as bad as he was at first," James added, more kindly. "That conscience of his used to bother him awfully whenever we had a little fun or did something out of the ordinary. Lately he has gotten more used to our ways, and we must have patience and help him along, for he is a valuable companion that we cannot afford to lose. I think sometimes that we do not have enough charity for him. For, you see, all of us have been raised differently."

"Yes, I think you grew up without any raising, James," George said.

At this remark the other boys laughed, even Byron, in spite of his feelings.

"Well, what I was saying," James continued when the merriment ceased, "was that our home training has not been at all the same. Byron has a mother that has done a great deal of preaching to him, and the fact is, it's hard to constantly sit under one kind of teaching and not be affected by the words of the preacher."

"No doubt some of these talks of his mother have taken such a firm hold upon him that it will not be possible for him to break away from them all at once. I think, however, that we can safely say that Byron is getting weaned away from his mother to some extent, and if we can only hold out, we'll be able to make him see as we do, and we must all have charity. What was that in our Sunday school lesson last Sunday about charity? 'Charity shall cover the multitude of sins,' wasn't it?"

"Now, James, you know very well that our teacher explained that Scripture in altogether a different way from that, and you cannot apply it in that way," Byron said indignantly. Then he added, "I can tell you this, boys if charity can be used to cover up sin, it will surely take a goodly pile to hide the deeds of tonight."

"You boys had better stop arguing and get down to business," Jason said. "The fire is in a fine condition now for roasting our chickens, and it's high time that they were on."

"I don't see anything in which to put them on," Byron remarked as he surveyed the room in a disdainful way.

"Of course, you don't," Jason continued. "That is to be produced by our own efforts. Just take that board and split off some pieces with your jackknife. Make your stick two or three feet long and sharpen it at one end. Then fasten a piece of chicken to it and hold it over the fire until it is done."

Again Byron tried desperately to hide his disgust, and presently each of the boys was endeavoring to follow out the instructions given them. Soon four sticks, with a piece of meat upon each, were being held over the fire, while the odor of the sizzling meat filled the room.

"If we only had a little salt to use as seasoning for our meat!" James remarked as he tested his meat to see whether it was done. "Why didn't I think and put a little in my pocket?"

"Don't chide yourself with forgetfulness, my friend. I usually carry such things with me as I know I will need in an emergency like this," said Jason, drawing from his pocket a small sack of salt. "These are little home comforts that we can't do without."

Much time and patience were required to cook the meat, but at last it was pronounced ready to eat. Still struggling with his feelings, Byron endeavored to eat the portion that he had roasted, but it was tough and raw. In fact, there was nothing tempting about it. As he looked about the dirty room and viewed the little group before him gnawing at the meat they held upon blackened sticks or in soiled fingers, and breathed into his lungs the foul odors of the musty room, his mind was carried back to the tempting feasts at home upon holidays and other occasions, that had often been prepared by his loving and thoughtful mother.

The table—covered with a snowy cloth and loaded with all the good things that the farm produced, graced by the huge platter with a juicy brown turkey or chicken upon it, and surrounded by a merry group of boys and girls, with mother in her accustomed place, and knives and forks to convey the food to their hungry mouths. This had always been a favorite scene. And now, as it came before him, he thought it was the most beautiful picture upon which he had ever looked. What a contrast! What a change! And in so short a time!

At home every advantage was awaiting him. He was not only a welcome member there, but his very presence was longed for. And yet he had chosen rather to be among thieves and robbers.

Again the scene changed. He though of when he was a small boy at mother's knee—innocent and free—with mother's hand fondly caressing him. Her admonitions to be good and to seek good company were clear and distinct, and the thought of the kiss upon his brow as he was tucked into bed almost brought the tears. Then he once more heard the echoes loud and distinct of that voice upon the foot log, warning him of dangers seen and unseen.

One piece of that chicken was all that he could possibly swallow. The food seemed to choke him, but it was not so with the other boys. They ate with a relish, and piece after piece disappeared. In fact, they did not stop eating until the last morsel of the food was gone. Filthy and vulgar stories were told during the meal, interspersed with an occasional witty remark about Byron or some reference to a former adventure in which they had barely escaped being caught.

When two hours of this sort of thing had passed, Byron became so weary that he could scarcely keep awake. It was not long past the midnight hour, and aside from the tramping and the excitement of the trip, he had put in a hard day of heavy toil in the field. He was weary and footsore, and as he thought of his downy pillows at home, his head sank forward lower and lower. Then he was asleep, dreaming of home and of mother.

"I wonder," Jason remarked, "if Byron said his prayers before he went to sleep, and if he is having very pleasant dreams?"

In an instant Byron was sitting up with all sleepiness driven far from him, wondering how long he had slept. The tempest of recollections that raged in his brain would be hard to describe.

"Sleep is a partner we can't do without," Jason continued. "Nothing can equal the influence of sleep upon the tired mind and body. But when sleep leaves us for a time, I know of a very good substitute; and here it is," he added, drawing from his pocket an old and much-used pipe. "This is the greatest comforter I have," he said as he proceeded to fill the pipe from the small bag of tobacco that he had taken from his pocket. "Whenever I'm tired a good smoke rests me; but the time when it's the greatest comfort to me is after a hearty meal. I only wish I had enough pipes to go around. But never mind, my friends, you shall each have a turn."

While the pipe was being passed from one to the other, Byron noticed that after smoking it each one assumed a dull and dazed expression, and he remembered his teacher's words when she explained the effects of tobacco upon the system. She said that the poison, or nicotine, in the tobacco worked on the system as to dull the senses. The seeming relief it produced was only temporary, and the poison not only produced a shock, but entered the most vital organs, doing great injury.

The strong odor from the pipe and the smoke that was constantly increasing in the room made him very uncomfortable. He did not want to take the horrid pipe in his mouth, but what was he to do when it came his turn? At last the pipe was offered to him. He took it, trying to think of some excuse to give it back. Not being able to make an excuse for not smoking and being unwilling to be laughed at, he braced himself for the task.

With the pipe held carelessly in his right hand, he joined freely in the conversation, endeavoring to avert attention and pretending now and then to smoke. As soon as he thought he could pass the detestable pipe on without inviting embarrassing remarks, he handed it the next fellow. Thus he avoided the deathly sick feeling that he had before experienced. If the boys noticed his actions, they said nothing.

It was not long until a pack of cards was produced, and game after game was played with them in the flickering firelight. Byron became really interested in the card games, though he was forced to battle with sleep. He was in a measure able to forget his surroundings, and did not so distinctly hear the voice of his conscience as he did when there was so little to take up his attention. As nothing was said about playing for money, the thought of gambling did not present itself in so repulsive a manner.

After several games had been played, George sprang up, and peering out into the darkness, exclaimed, "Boys, I really believe it's getting light in the east! We had better be making tracks for home if we don't want to be caught by Mr. Sun."

He had scarcely finished speaking when a cock in a distant farm yard began to crow. On hearing it, Jason sprang to his feet and said excitedly, "Well, I should say so! If we don't get out of here at once, we'll be sure to be seen, and then we'll catch it!"

The boys took no time to change the appearance of the room nor to put out the remains of the fire, but quickly fled out into the darkness. They followed the same course that had been traveled earlier in the evening and were soon wending their way along the riverbank and out again upon the highway. While passing the Sibley house, Jason whispered, "We are none too soon, boys. To be seen around here will not be good medicine for us. The best thing to do is to hustle home as lively as we can and to be sure that no grass grows under our feet along the way."

"Humph, you must have imbibed some of Byron's doctrine," James remarked in a low tone.

"Well, his preaching may not be so bad," Jason answered, "for some of these things we've done tonight will no doubt be found out before long. The first question about the matter will be, 'Who did them?' and for us to be seen together at this hour of the morning will be a pretty hard thing to explain away."

The boys separated at the crossroads—George and Jason going in one direction, and James and Byron in another. As they were hastening down the road toward the farmer's house, James remarked, "It will not be safe for us to try to enter the house at this hour. It might arouse unnecessary suspicion. We'll slip around to the hay barn, which is never locked, and creep in there."

So with great caution they entered the gate that led into the farmer's yard, and, softly slipping around the house, they entered an old log barn, where the hay for the horses and cattle was kept. Then they mounted a ladder that led up to the loft above. As they laid down upon the hay, James said, "Here we can get a couple of hours sleep at least before breakfast."

It was no trouble for James to fall asleep, but with Byron it was different. He had never before slept in a barn, and then once more he had to listen to the voice that had troubled him at the river. But from sheer exhaustion he at last closed his eyes. The incidents of the day passed before him, but they became more and more indistinct until he forgot them altogether and slept.

When he awoke, the farmer was below, attending to his morning chores, and the sunlight was streaming in through the wide cracks between the logs of which the barn was made. At first Byron did not realize where he was, and his surroundings appeared so strange that he wondered if he was having a strange dream or a nightmare. But he soon realized that it was all too true and that it was really Sunday morning.

"What are they doing at home?" he wondered. "Mother is no doubt preparing breakfast and thinking of her wayward boy, perhaps praying at this very moment. Very soon it will be time for the morning worship, when the family will be gathered together. Mother will take the Bible and read a chapter. Then as they silently kneel to pray, she will remember each one of her children. What will she say when she comes to my name?"

He could almost hear the words pouring from her troubled soul, "O Lord, be with Byron, wherever he may be this morning. Bless my wayward boy and shield him from the many snares that Satan has prepared for his feet. Without Thy sustaining grace, O Lord, my heart would give way beneath its burden this morning. O God! how I love my boy! How I long for his salvation! Have pity and compassion upon him for Jesus' sake! Give me strength, dear Father, to bear up under this new trial, and bring to my boy's mind his former teaching. Talk to him, Lord, through his conscience and bring him safely home to me again. Have pity and compassion upon him for Jesus' sake."

Rising upon his elbow, Byron glanced to see if James had wakened, but found that he was sleeping soundly. Byron settled back once more into the nest that he had made in the hay, and tried to get more sleep. But the noises of the farmer moving about below kept him awake, and the various greetings that the different animals gave their owner when he approached them with their morning meal brought remembrances of his own neglected duties at home.

The sound of streams of milk pouring into empty milk pails renewed his thoughts of mother. He would not be there to help her with the milking, and it would be difficult for her to finish her other duties in time for Sunday school.

When the squealing of the pigs had died away in the pen adjoining the log barn and the farmer had returned up the gravel walk to the house, all was once more quiet, and for another hour James continued to sleep.

At last Byron heard him exclaim, "Whew! Is it really morning? Say, but I've had a good sleep. How did you rest, old boy? Pretty fine, I suppose; and did you have peaceful dreams?" Not waiting for a reply, James quickly arose, saying, "If two boys want any breakfast, they had better make haste and get into the house. Things will be cold now, I expect."

"It would make little difference to me if I had no breakfast," Byron said. "For my part, I am not in the least hungry. This staying up all night has just taken all of the life and ambition out of me. I don't feel a bit like myself, and such a weight and burden has come over me since last evening that I am perfectly miserable. I thought that perhaps when I had slept some I would feel better, and in one sense I do. But, oh! I don't feel as I used to. James, when I think of my unkind remarks to Mother last night, it almost breaks my heart."

"Oh, never mind your feelings, Byron," James said in a more encouraging tone of voice than he had been using of late. "You'll feel all right when you've had a good hearty breakfast and a strong cup of coffee to stimulate you! Some of the things last night were just a little new to you and were no doubt exciting; but when your nerves quiet down a bit, you'll be yourself again."

"Well, what you say may be true, James, but what are you going to tell the folks in the house? How will you explain our being out last night?"

"Just leave that to me, Byron," James answered. "I have many times had to make explanations, and I think I'm equal to the occasion this morning. But we had better be moving on at once, as it's getting late."

Descending a ladder, they left the barn through a rear door, and then snuck along behind a fence until they reached the road, so that they could enter the yard through the gate in front of the house. As they entered the yard, the farmer noticed them, but he did not suspect that they had spent a part of the night in the barn.

"It seems to me, boys, that you are rather late, or early, I do not know which you would call it, in getting back from the post office," he said rather gruffly.

Reaching into his pocket, James brought forth the mail that he had received the night before, saying, "We had intended to come directly home from the post office, but after we left the store, George was taken with some kind of sick spell. It was quite a while before he could walk at all, and when we finally got started, Byron and I had to help him along. We went with him all the way to his home and saw him safely in bed. By that time it was so late that we didn't like to come home and disturb you, and as they gave us an urgent invitation to stay all night, we decided to do so. George was so much better this morning that we came over here as soon as we could."

As James finished these remarks, he glanced quickly at Byron and winked as if to say, "I fixed that up all right, didn't I?"

Little was said during breakfast, and as soon as possible after it was over, the boys prepared to leave for Sunday school. They planned on attending the services at the little chapel that day, not because they wished to learn more about the Lord and salvation, but because they knew that they would be expected to be there and that many difficult questions would be asked if they were not.

Sunday school did not begin until ten o'clock, and as they had plenty of time they did not hasten on their way. Neither was in a talkative mood, so Byron had an opportunity to think, and many peculiar thoughts surged through his mind. He remembered the kindness of his teacher, a motherly, middle-aged woman, as from time to time she had taught his class. How sweet and good she had appeared while explaining the lesson and illustrating it by stories taken either from the Bible or from life!

One of these stories now came to his mind. It was of Jonah, the Bible truant. He remembered that she had pictured Jonah's stubborn and rebellious spirit, and had described the trouble and disaster he brought upon himself through his unwillingness to obey God.

He did not want to be like Jonah. He would choose to be more brave and noble. Jonah's course had often been a source of wonderment to him, and he reasoned that it was foolish and unnecessary. But how about his own? Jonah sinned only by turning from his duty and trying to run away from God, but he, Byron, not only had turned from duty and from God, but had committed sins that were really crimes.

Jonah, he remembered having heard her say, was really a good man, and wanted to do right. God had commanded him to warn the people of their danger—to inform them that if they did not repent they would be destroyed. Jonah had been severely punished because of his disobedience alone, and Byron wondered what would be done to those who not only disobeyed but committed crimes as well.

The sight of his mother's carriage and horse tied near the chapel door told plainly that she was there in her accustomed seat. In order to take his place in his class, he must pass directly in front of her. How he dreaded to look into her eyes, which thing he knew he would be almost obliged to do. Many a time he had entered that door with a heart as light and happy as a bird, but now it was different.

She was there as Byron had expected, and as he looked into that patient face, so kind and pure, he was unable to return the smile with which she greeted him. With shame and guilt burning into his soul, he longed to hide himself. Heavy weights seemed to be fastened to his feet, and his heart was as lead. If only he could recall the cruel words of the evening before! Dropping his eyes to the floor, he walked as quickly as possible down the aisle and slipped into the seat beside James. Then began a tempest more fierce than any that had ever raged in his soul.

"The Lord's Secret" was the subject of the lesson, and the memory verse was, "My doctrine is not mine, but his that sent me." As the teacher explained the Jews' question in regard to the wisdom of Jesus and applied the memory verse, she said, "The secret of the Lord is very simple if anyone will open his heart to receive it. Now, Jesus came into the world to show men and women how to be good and happy. It was a very simple lesson that He wanted to teach them—the difference between right and wrong—and because of its simplicity the people who had been so long striving to solve it, thinking it was a difficult problem, could not easily understand. They were of the opinion that in order to get anything out of the Scriptures one must have much learning, and, knowing that Jesus had not enjoyed many educational privileges, they considered themselves safe in saying that He was not a scholar.

"In His answer Jesus told them that it did not require earthly wisdom in this instance, for His teacher was God. And that all who would know of His secret must be willing to be taught in the same way."

She then told her class a little story that she had read. In the story the human heart was compared to a box securely locked and hidden in a large house. The first, or outside, door of this house opened into an entryway, into which strangers were admitted. The second door admitted acquaintances into halls and parlors. The third door opened into the living room, and here relatives and close friends were entertained. The next opened into the chamber where none but the nearest and dearest could come. Aside from all these, there was still another door, which opened into the closet containing the secret box.

This box represented the heart, which contains the secret thoughts and desires of the soul, the best and noblest, as well as the lowest and basest. Now, only God's eye could see into the heart and discern man's true character. But there is a day coming, Byron's teacher said, when the heart will be opened, and as the husks are stripped from the corn and the shell removed from the kernel, so the thoughts of our hearts will be revealed as they really are.

Then she retold the story of the aged men who were walking upon the seashore viewing the wreckage. One of them was evidently a sailor and a person well acquainted with that part of the country, for he could explain something about most of the rubbish with which the coast was strewn.

As they came to the keel of a huge ship half buried in the sand, he said, "I remember well the night this came ashore. She was a fine ship and was well manned, and the master's chart plainly described the bar on which she struck. He could have missed it, but he thought he could come a little closer than the map stated and still miss it. He tried it, but was caught in a storm, and his vessel was lost."

Coming to another wreck, he said, "And I remember, too, when this bark was heaving her anchor, one fine morning, with every promise of a prosperous voyage. Her captain thought she would not need a pilot, and the result was that she, too, came ashore. My friend," the old man continued, "as I look up and down this rocky coast and view the wrecks with which it is strewn, whose history I know so well, I am made sad indeed, and life seems to be full of clouds and storms."

"When I read this story, boys," the teacher said, "I thought of the many young men starting out upon life's voyage. Some of them are wise enough to take a Pilot with them, but do not listen to His voice and at the risk of their lives and friends venture too close to the bar and are shipwrecked. How I wish that everyone could realize his danger when he turns away from the warnings of his conscience and ventures too close to dangerous places. The conscience warns of danger, but its power to help is useless when its instruction is not obeyed. Like an abused and slighted friend, it will in time become wounded and silenced.

"I wish, boys, that you would each learn the great secret contained in our lesson today that Jesus endeavored to teach the people. If you will follow the directions that are laid down in God's chart, the Bible, and let Jesus be your Pilot, you not only will be able to plow through the foaming billows, but will land in the quiet waters of the haven of success, carrying with you rich cargoes of joy and happiness. Otherwise you are in constant danger of either being wrecked or carried away in the tide of sin and wickedness.

"How sad it would be, when God calls you home, should you find that your life had been wasted; that God's design for you had not been fulfilled because you refused to follow the instructions of the chart or obey the counsel of the Pilot. Heed them, boys. God wants you to have a purpose in life that will reveal the best that is in you. A strong Christian character and a distinct purpose are what God desired above all things else."

The entire lesson made a deep impression upon Byron. He was still thinking seriously upon it when he felt a gentle touch upon his shoulder. Looking up, he saw that it was his mother, saying, "I hope, boys, that you have had a pleasant time together, and that you enjoyed yourselves last night."

He felt a choking sensation as he tried to answer, and could not think of anything to say. But his companion, seeing his predicament, spoke for him.

"Oh, yes," James said, "we had a very nice time. Byron was a little late in getting there, but we spent a very pleasant evening with the family and in reading over our Sunday school lesson."

Somewhat recovering himself from his surprise, Byron endeavored to join in the conversation, but it was with difficulty that he did so. He could think of little to say, and what he did say had an awkward and uncertain meaning. His mother did not press him any farther with questions; and as she was ready to leave for home, Byron bade James goodbye and entered the carriage beside her.

CHAPTER VII
STRANDED

It was a beautiful day. The little birds had finished their morning songs and were busy with other duties, but occasionally some songster in a clump of trees near the road cheered the passersby with his music. As Byron rode home from Sunday school with his mother, he tried hard to forget his cruel words to her and what had followed. But, try as he would, the remembrance of these things persisted in returning to his troubled mind. Would his mother talk to him about it when they got home? How could he answer her?

However, his mother never mentioned what had happened. During the entire week she bestowed upon him the same affection that she had in former days, and he also heard nothing from the boys; but everything about the place seemed changed. The house, the yard, the well, the garden, and even the horses and the barn seemed different to him. Yet they were the same—the change was in himself.

In every way his mother was a wonder to him. He had never known her to be so kind. At meals she placed special dainties on his plate, and when he had finished his day's work she greeted him with pleasant and endearing words. The chapters she read during the worship hour were full of deep meaning, and the prayers she offered sank into his heart like arrows.

Once after prayer he felt that he must go to her and unburden his heart and beg forgiveness for the way he had spoken to her. But the suggestion quickly came that it would be better not to do it. It would only make bad matters worse, for it was not really necessary. Then he wondered if anyone had found out about what had happened on Saturday night. Thus the week slipped away, and Sunday morning came again.

Byron opened his eyes and beheld the warm rays of sunlight streaming into his room through the open window. He felt thankful that his surroundings were different from what they were the week before. Then a call from the stairway reminded him that breakfast was nearly ready. He had no time to lose if he were to get to Sunday school on time.

Promptness was a thing that had always been taught in Byron's home. When attending school, which was some distance away, he had never had any tardy marks against him, and the family had always made a special effort to be at Sunday school on time. On this particular morning Byron was eager to get started. He was anxious to see James and George and to learn how things were going.

To Byron's surprise, when he reached the chapel, the boys were not there. Perhaps they had been detained, he thought, and would come in later; so he carefully watched the door for a long time. So interested was he to see them enter that he paid little attention to the lesson or to what the teacher was saying. When the school was dismissed, he asked some of the boys if they knew why James and George were absent. But none of them knew.

He walked silently out into the yard, and after looking up and down the road, hoping that the boys would appear, he sat down in the carriage. Soon the preaching service began. Byron heard the singing, but he did not care to go inside. He was disappointed because the boys did not come, and he wanted to be alone.

"What a relief it would be," he said to himself, "to know what has hindered them! It is certainly unusual, for they are nearly always at Sunday school and are generally on time." Then a sudden fear gripped his heart. Could it be possible that anything had happened? Had some of their reckless deeds of the week before been discovered and traced to the guilty ones? Why was there such a choking sensation in his throat, and such a feeling and expectancy of danger in his mind? Had not James repeatedly assured him that there was no reason to be afraid? Yes, he had—but, then, had not Jason told them both that there was cause for real carefulness as well as fear? Jason and George had seemed to understand the necessity of covering the deeds of that awful night, and they were both older and more experienced than James. These and many similar thoughts troubled Byron as he sat there alone in the carriage. He could easily have listened to a part of the sermon, as the carriage was close to the open windows and doors, but his mind was too busily occupied with other things.

What made Byron start so suddenly, and what caused him to tremble so violently? Two men, in a covered buggy, had turned into the churchyard, had alighted, and were approaching the carriage in which Byron was sitting. It was no uncommon thing for him to see these men, for he was well acquainted with them both. One of them was Farmer Davis. He was the owner of the house whose windows the boys had broken by throwing stones and clubs, and of the orchard in which George had destroyed the apple trees.

The men greeted him with a pleasant smile and spoke very kindly to him; but as they talked he became more and more uneasy. He felt that something was surely to happen soon, and his conscience was again talking with him. He struggled to be brave, but he could not look either of the men in the face. His guilty conscience alone would have condemned him.

Suddenly the conversation ceased. During the silence that followed, Byron felt that the terrible moment had arrived. Although his eyes were riveted on the ground, he knew that both men were looking him squarely in the face.

"Where were you, Byron," Mr. Davis asked, "on Saturday night one week ago?"

Byron felt the color leave his cheek. His throat became dry and parched. He tried to say that he had spent the night with James, and that they had remained in the house all evening, but his words felt strange and weak.

The men did not seem surprised; but Mr. Davis continued, "Now, Byron, you might as well tell us the truth, for your guilty look has betrayed you. You know very well that what you've said isn't so. We have known you since you were a small boy, and we know that your mother is a good woman and has tried to bring you up in the right way. We know, too, that of late you have been keeping company with boys whom you have no business to be with. These boys have influenced you and have encouraged you to do things you would not have otherwise done. This has been so noticeable that others have spoken about it. You are breaking your mother's heart and bringing disgrace and reproach upon a respectable family.

"Now, the way of the transgressor is hard, and you will have to give an answer for some of the things you have done. You say that you spent the night with James and that you were not out of the house all evening. Now, Byron, why do you say that?"

Byron tried to answer, but could not. The words seemed to die in his throat as the pangs of guilt pierced his heart. He would have given anything to be rid of that awful feeling.

"You see," Mr. Davis went on, in a voice which showed that he knew and understood a great deal about the matter, "the facts in the case are these: I happened to be in the post office that evening and distinctly remember noticing you and James and another boy come in to ask for mail. I saw you reluctantly take the cigar that James gave you, and when it was lighted place it between your lips. Later I was told by another man that he had seen you going away from church in the same company, except that Jason White had gone with you. Now, you were seen at these places, and still you claim to have spent the entire evening with James at his home. There must be some cause for your making a statement like that. Why did you do it?"

Byron was still speechless. He could not answer.

"You were in the company of those three boys that night, and you know just what you did," Mr. Davis continued when he saw that Byron was not willing to confess himself. "As soon as your evil deeds were discovered, an investigation was started. You four boys were suspected at once, and every bit of evidence that we have collected points that way. You are guilty, and the best thing for you to do is to acknowledge it and to take your medicine. Now, if you can tell the truth, we will intercede in your behalf, as we believe that you have been influenced and have been thus led into trouble."

Byron could stand no more. With quivering lips and shining eyes, he acknowledged his guilt and pled for mercy. He ended his pitiful story by saying, "Oh, do not tell my poor mother! It will break her heart. She warned me faithfully, but I would not heed her advice, and now it has come to this." And burying his face in his hands he sobbed, "What will Mother say? How can I ever face her again?"

The two men talked kindly to Byron, but let him know that his mother must be told. The offense was so grave that it would be necessary for the law to have its course, and that the boys must suffer the consequences.

"We are going now," Mr. Davis gravely said, "to visit an officer of the law, and you will hear from this later. My advice to you would be to tell a straightforward story. It will certainly be better for you in the end if you do."

As the two men untied their horse and drove away Byron watched them in a bewildered manner until they had disappeared.

"O God!" he cried, realizing his fate, "what shall I do? I can never face this!"

He thought of running away, but wondered where he could go. His mother would find it out, anyway, and why make her suffer any more than she must? With teeth set firmly together, he said to himself, "I might as well face it one time as another." With this thought uppermost in his mind he jumped from the carriage and, going into the chapel, dropped into the first empty seat. In a few minutes the service ended.

As Byron sat still, wondering what his mother would say when she had learned all, his cousin came to him and invited Byron to go home with him. "Oh, here is my chance," he thought. "If I go to his home, I won't have to tell Mother myself. Someone else will surely tell her before I get home tonight."

He got permission from his mother to spend the afternoon at his cousin's home, promising to return home before sundown.

What an afternoon that was! A good dinner had been prepared by his aunt, but he had no relish for it. His cousin proposed games and amusements of various kinds, in which the two boys had often engaged, and even a trip down to the river, but nothing seemed to interest him. He was thoroughly miserable. At last, seeing the sun sinking to rest, he started home. As he walked along, he wondered again and again what was awaiting him there. Had Mother heard? How could he meet her? What questions would she first ask him? These and many other things came to his mind as he wended his way homeward.

When he came in sight of his home, he stopped, and his courage fell. How could he ever enter that place again? he thought. He felt that he was worse than an outcast, for he had abused and misused his rights and was no longer worthy to share the comforts of home. The story of the prodigal son came to his mind. How like that miserable fellow he felt himself!

Summoning all his remaining courage, he again pressed on. The door opened. There stood his mother, her hand still clinging to the knob as if for support. One glance at her pale, tear-stained face told him that she already knew the dreadful story. The awful look of sorrow spoke more plainly than words could have done, but beneath her sorrow, he could see that there was still the same tender love.

Springing forward, Byron clasped her in his arms, saying, "O Mother! you have heard the story, haven't you? Can you ever love and respect your wayward boy again? Can you ever have any confidence in him?"

And the two poor, wounded hearts poured out their grief together.

"O my boy," at last his mother cried, "has it come to this? You have indeed broken my heart! If it were not for the comfort and strength I am now receiving from above, I could never stand this."

"Yes, Mother," Byron said in a low tone, "It has come to this! Can you forgive me? Oh, say that you can!" And then, in the gathering gloom, he told his mother the tale of his sorrow and distress.

When his mother had recovered herself sufficiently, she told Byron that, two hours before, the men who had talked to him in the churchyard had come to her home and told her all about the trouble.

"Oh! you cannot imagine, Byron, how I felt!" she exclaimed, sobbing again. "It pierced my heart like poisoned arrows, and I have suffered terribly!"

"Yes, Mother," Byron answered gently. "I do know something about your feelings; for I have passed through an experience that I shall never forget! Your prayers have followed me all the way! When I left you that night at the gate, with those cruel words ringing in my ears, you told me that you would pray for me. Well, I had a strange experience that night." Then Byron told her all about the voice that spoke to him as he crossed the river and stood upon the foot log.

"O my boy!" his mother exclaimed, "God is surely talking to you through His Spirit. He wants to save you from your sinful ways and deliver your soul from all guilt and condemnation. The voice that you heard on the foot log was more than your conscience alone; it was God's Holy Spirit, in answer to prayer, striving to make you see and understand your duty toward your Creator and to keep you out of danger. Jesus wants to come into your heart and make it His abode, and God will give you His Holy Spirit to guide you if only you will let Him."

"I know it, Mother, and I long to be free from sin, but this affair that I am in is something awful, and I must face it!" he said, burying his face in his hands.

"Yes, my boy, you will have to meet it. Mr. Davis said that as soon as he could locate the other boys an officer of the law would come to arrest you." Then rising, and lighting a lamp, she continued, "Aren't you hungry, Byron? Come and have some food."

The two walked together into the dining room, and while Byron ate a light supper his mother sat beside him and listened to the remaining details of the sad story. At last she said, "You must go to bed now, my son, for you may be called for in the night." And with a goodnight kiss they parted at the stairway.

Going to his room, Byron made hasty preparations for bed, and throwing himself upon it, gave vent to his feelings. The tears that he had struggled to suppress, because he did not think it manly to cry, flowed freely now, and he round the relief that nature gives to grieving hearts.

How dark the future, at this moment, appeared to this wayward young man, no one but those who have a like experience can comprehend. He felt that all happiness was gone out of his life and that it would be impossible ever to live down a record so dark, so black! He could not bear to think of what the next few hours would bring forth.

If only he had listened to his dear mother's advice! If only he had heeded the warnings of his conscience, he would have been spared all of this! In utter despair he buried his face in his pillow. "O God!" he cried form the agony of his heart, "what shall I—what can I—do?" The wail had scarcely died upon the night air, when he arose upon his elbow to listen.

He heard a sound of wheels in the distance coming in the direction of his home. Could it be, oh! could it be the officers? Yes. The wagon had stopped. Feet were walking upon the graveled walk below. Mother had opened the door. He heard voices, but the words were indistinct.

Upon the mantle in the dining room the old clock was sounding the hour of nine, and Byron heard the hall door gently opening and someone coming up the stairs. It was Mother! She was coming to break the news as softly as possible. Stopping beside his bed, she clasped him to herself, kissing him again and again. For a moment neither mother nor son uttered a word; but as he felt the hot tears falling upon his face and the heaving of her bosom, Byron knew something of his mother's suffering.

At last, as if in a dream, Byron heard her saying, "An officer is below, waiting for you, Byron. You must dress at once and go down. It's hard, but you must face it. You will probably be taken for trial, and I cannot go, but your older brother will go with you. I'm going to give you enough money to pay your fine, however much it will be. If they will let you off that way, perhaps you can return with your brother tomorrow.

"But now, my boy, there is one thing I must ask of you, and it is this: when you are put upon the witness stand, be truthful. Tell everything just as it happened and do not try to shield yourself, no matter what the consequences may be. Never mind what the boys may say or do; speak the truth and let the law have its course. It will be hard for us all, but we must submit.

"While I shall not be with you, Byron, remember that I am praying for you, and I'm sure God in His mercy will come to your rescue in this trying hour. You remember what I told you of the voyage that you were starting upon. You are stranded now, my boy, upon the shoals that Satan has prepared for unwary souls; and because you failed to properly prepare for the journey, your former reputation will indeed be shipwrecked. But don't be discouraged. Jesus extends a lifeline to the lost, and if you will look you can easily find it."

Then kissing him on the brow again, she said, "I will go now, and you must come down immediately or the men will be coming up after you."

Byron did not move until the door to the dining room below had closed behind his mother. Reluctantly, then, he arose, then dressed quickly, and was soon descending the stairs over which he had so often traveled before. Where would he spend the nights that were to follow this one?

As he entered the dining room, he was seized with a choking sensation. He knew practically nothing of the law and its officers and of their methods of dealing with their prisoners, but he had at last made up his mind to take his mother's advice. He would follow her directions as closely as it as possible for him to do.

Mustering all of his immature manly powers, he stepped into the presence of those whom he most dreaded to see. There was no unnecessary delay or words. The officer was prepared, and, drawing forth a paper from his pocket, he began at once to read from its contents, and after finishing it he said, "Byron, you are now under arrest."

Solemn words indeed were these in the ears of Byron. He felt himself a great criminal. He looked at his mother as she stood beside him and realized in part what she was suffering. He saw the great tears running down her cheeks, and remembered when she had said, just a few hours before, "O my boy! you have broken my heart!" It seemed too true. He was indeed stranded, and he felt that only a divine power could release him.

For a moment no one spoke; then the officer broke the painful silence. "I had intended, Byron," he said, "to take you with me, but I have decided not to do so. You will be placed upon your honor to appear at the place for your trial and can come with your brother later tonight. I must go and arrest the other boys, and as soon as I can get them it will be necessary for you to be there."

Three hours later, when his brother called to him from the gate, Byron arose and went out into the night. A moment later he heard his mother's footsteps behind him. No words were spoken. After a tender embrace and a loving kiss she helped him into the carriage, and the two brothers were soon driving out onto the highway.

The hour of the night, their mission, his mother at the gate, and the moon above looking down upon them made the scene very impressive to Byron. The picture that was there stamped upon his mind was never erased.

Chapter VIII
Shipwrecked

Only a little more than a week had passed since Byron left his mother standing beside that same gateway. She pleaded with him then, but her pleading had been in vain. He had not heeded her advice. He had cast it aside and almost ignored it. He had thought he knew best. Now he could see that his mother was right. Now all was changed.

Oh, if only he could undo the deeds of the past few weeks! But the days that were past could not be recalled. He must suffer now for his misdeeds! How dark was the future! Would he be permitted to return home after the trial, or would he be taken to the jail? Would the money that his mother had given his brother be of any service? These and similar thoughts filled his mind as the carriage rolled along.

As the carriage neared the river, Byron could see in the distance the outline of the old house in which the boys had spent that eventful night. As he crossed the bridge, he saw the moonbeams sparkling in the water below and thought of the foot log farther up the stream. The voice that had spoken to him in the lonely forest on that fatal night was still pleading in the same tender manner. He longed to cry out to God for pardon, for at last he realized that it was God's Holy Spirit that was talking to him in answer to his mother's prayer. He longed to live a new and different life that he might be not only an example to his friends but an encouragement to his sorrowing mother.

During most of the journey the two brothers rode in silence, as each was busy with his own thoughts. When they reached their destination, each drew a deep sigh; but it was not the sigh of relief, for neither one was glad. They realized what was before them, and Byron felt his strength and courage failing every moment.

The village in which the squire lived consisted of only about half a dozen weather-beaten houses. But this fact did not interest the brothers; they were looking for the squire's office, which did not take long to find. They tied their horse in front of his house, they knocked on the door.

The squire was not at all pleased about being disturbed at so early an hour. Leading them into the living room—which was also his office—he gruffly bade them be seated. Then he went back to his bed to rest until the others should arrive.

In the stillness that followed, Byron tried to imagine what would be the outcome of the next few hours. He shuddered over the prospect, and again fear, such as he had never before experienced, took hold of him. He thought of the squire's stern features and doubted that he would show any mercy.

As the sound of heavy breathing in the bedroom reached his ears, he thought of his own soft bed at home and of Mother; dear, patient Mother! Was she asleep? Had she had any rest? One thing he knew, and that was that she had been praying for him. This thought quieted his fears, and he wondered how much her prayers would help. The minutes passed wearily by. Slowly his eyes began to droop. Then sleep caused Byron to forget that he was not resting upon his own pillow at home.

When he awoke, the sun was peeping over the treetops. It was a beautiful morning. A merry little songster in the yard warbled forth its praise to its Creator for placing such beauty upon the earth. The notes sounded as mockery in Byron's ears. Would he ever be happy again? Would his burden of guilt and sin ever be lifted? Could he ever again feel himself an innocent boy?

Another hour passed. Still the brothers waited for the arrival of the others who were to have a part in the trial. Suddenly there was a noise at the gate, and, looking out the window, Byron saw the officer who had arrested him the night before. And with him were James and George.

With keenest interest Byron watched them approach the house. He realized that they had not met since the night of their evil deeds, but he was quite sure that by now they knew of his confession, and he wondered how they would act toward him and what they would say when they came in.

The squire had also heard the click of the gate. He arose, and dressing quickly, was soon at the door to receive them. As the three entered the room, Byron saw them glance quickly in his direction.

When his eyes met theirs, he read anything but sympathy and love in their expression. He thought of James' promised friendship in times of trouble. James had said that he not only would help and stand by him, but would be his right hand man.

Faithful companion indeed! If Byron wanted help now he must look for it from a very different source. He felt the separation more keenly than if words had passed between them. These boys would never again want to associate with him, and he did not desire their companionship any longer. He had at least one true friend, and that was his mother. He knew that she would stand by him no matter what might happen.

In a short time two other rigs drove up in front of the house and five more men entered the squire's office. One of these men was the prosecuting attorney, and two others the neighbors to whom Byron had talked the day before in the churchyard. All had a smile and a kindly word for Byron.

Presently the officers of the law collected in one corner of the room and conversed in low tones for several minutes. Byron listened with an eagerness that he had never before known. He wanted to learn all the facts in the case as soon as possible, and he wished to know why Jason was not present. Shortly he heard an officer, speaking in a louder tone, say that he had gone to arrest Jason but had failed. In some way word that the officers were coming had reached him, and he had left and could not be found. They continued to talk among themselves for some time and then motioned to the other men to join them. Again they spoke in tones too low to be heard by the boys.

The moments crept slowly by for the prisoners, but at last the scene was changed. The squire, after producing some writing material, seated himself with the others around a table, and then the prosecuting attorney remarked, "It is now time to commence the trial."

When the preliminary address had been given, Byron was called forward as the first witness. In spite of his efforts to be calm, he could scarcely control himself. He trembled so violently that it was with difficulty that he answered the questions.

It was not strange that he was so affected: the prosecuting attorney was none other than the storekeeper to whom Byron had sold the eggs on his way to the mill. While the officers had talked among themselves, the whole experience with the eggs had come vividly before him—first the plan that James had concocted to bring the boys more spending money, next the temptation, then the theft, and last of all the disposal of the eggs. His mother's words about deception growing in the heart, spoken to him when she punished him for deceiving her about the planting of the beans, had been fulfilled.

He had also remembered the little vision that had come before him as he stood in front of the little store—the vision of the gambling party who had changed into the forms of James, George, his cousin, and himself. And he recalled the miller's story. "Ah," he thought, "if only I had tried to change my course and had made my wrongs right before things came to this! I could easily have replaced the eggs or have taken them to Mother, and I should have been saved all this trouble."

Every step in the wrong direction had made his return more difficult. There was not a shadow of a reason for the course that he had taken. He had not even the excuse that the miller had given in regard to the poor widow. A great cloud of darkness seemed to have suddenly arisen and threatened him with utter destruction.

He was indeed sorry now; but as a captain, realizing that the rudder of his vessel is broken, looks out upon the distant horizon and sees the storm approaching, so Byron looked into the faces of those before him in this terrific storm of life.

After he had answered the questions, he was told to make a statement of all that he and the other boys had done. He instantly remembered his mother's advice—to speak the truth in everything and to tell the particulars just as nearly as he could. "No doubt she is praying for me at this very moment," he thought. Inspired by this thought and the remembrance of her words, he told the story in a straightforward manner. As he confessed one thing after another, the look of terror left his face.

When he had finished speaking, he glanced toward the boys. Their opinion of him was still visible, but he no longer cared. He did not now desire their friendship, and experience had taught him what kind of help to expect from them in time of trouble.

He was asked a few more questions, and then James and George were in turn called forward. Both denied the charges brought against them and said that all of Byron's talk was false and was made to get them into trouble.

When asked to tell where they had been on the Saturday night in question, each made up a story of his own; but when they were questioned more closely, their own words proved them guilty. One witness tried to testify in their favor, but his testimony was of no avail.

Then the prosecutor made a talk, in which he gave the boys some good, sound advice, and admonished them to abide by the law if they did not want to suffer the penalties that were attached to its violation. Next a large law book was produced, and the sentence for a crime such as they had committed was read. Besides the fine, there was a certain length of time to be spent in prison.

As Byron listened, it seemed all hope had left him. His breath came in gasps, and his face grew white. He had hoped that when the fine was paid he would be permitted to return home. He wanted to make amends for his wrongs and to help his poor mother forget her sorrow. What would she say? Would he ever be able to rise above a prison sentence? Could he ever take his stand in the world again?

He felt a great relief when the officer again rose and in solemn tones addressed the boys. "James and George will have to suffer the full extent of the law. They will be punished not only for the crime but for trying to shield themselves. But with Byron we will make a difference. He has been truthful, and he seems to be sorry not only for what has happened, but for having been led into bad company. When he has paid the fine he can return to his home and to his mother."

At this, Mr. Davis, who had been strangely quiet, arose, and going to Byron, grasped his hand and spoke encouragingly to him. Then they all passed out of the squire's office and were soon driving away in different directions. Byron, driving home with his brother, looked back over his shoulder and saw the officer with James and George disappearing at a turn in the road. He realized that just as they were passing from his sight they were also passing out of his life. Never again would he be led about in sin by these boys.

His thoughts and desires were so changed that he longed only for a pure and upright life and for the happiness and satisfaction that such a life gives. There was nothing for which he cared to live but to prove his love for his mother and to counteract his past actions toward her and the others whom he had wronged. The awful weight of his sin seemed to hold him down so securely that he could find no relief.

As the two brothers rode along side by side, they had little to say to each other, merely making an occasional remark about the crops or the weather. Neither mentioned the events of the past few hours. Higher and higher the sun rose until they realized it was nearing noon. They were glad when they could see in the distance the outline of their home.

How changed everything appeared to Byron as they approached their home. Changed and beautiful! Byron at last realized what home meant to him and saw the value of friends—noble and true friends, who would not turn away from him in times of trouble and distress. Would Mother see them and be at the gate to welcome them? Straining his eyes, he thought he could see someone at the very spot where she had stood when he had spoken those cruel words upon that fatal night.

Yes, Mother was there—dear, patient, sorrowing Mother—with lines of grief and distress written plainly upon a face that was lighted by a smile of welcome! Byron could now read beneath the smile and was beginning to understand the effort his mother was making to be brave. He noticed that the sleepless hours of the previous night had left their imprint on her features, and as he thought of the hours of mental suffering that she had borne, he wondered if he could ever make atonement.

Almost before the horse had stopped, she was beside the carriage, reaching for her boy, and as Byron threw himself into her outstretched arms, unbidden tears began to flow.

"Oh, tell me all about everything," she said, when at last she could speak, brushing away the scalding tears. "Tell me how the trial came out!"

Her eldest son said, "Byron is greatly favored, but the other boys have been sent to jail. Go with Mother, Byron, and tell her all about it. She would rather have you tell her, I'm sure." So while his brother attended to the horse, Byron entered the house with his mother.

"O my son!" she said as she led her boy to an easy chair, "you don't know how glad I am to have you at home with me again. I prayed and plead last night that God would, if possible, spare you from prison and bring you back to us again, and He has answered my prayer!"

Then, clasping his hand in hers, she listened to his broken account of all that occurred while he was away.

"And, Mother dear," he added, "I knew that you were praying for me. I felt the influence of your prayers, and I, too, feel that God has heard and answered prayer. I know you have often prayed for me, and I have felt the effect of those prayers many times. Oh, Mother, I feel that I have not only been disobedient and have filled your heart with sorrow, but have brought an awful disgrace upon the family

76

name. Can you forgive it all? I feel unworthy of being called your son any more. My life is unhappy. My sins rise up as mountains before me, and, oh, how I wish I could be free and feel myself the same innocent boy I was when I used to bow in prayer at your knee. The voice that you called the Holy Spirit has spoken to me, and since that time I have found no peace of mind. The things I used to enjoy and take pleasure in I have no desire for now. A change has already come into my life, but, oh, what a burden and weight I feel all the time! How I long to be rid of it! Do you suppose, Mother, there is any help for me?"

"Yes, indeed, my son," his mother said as she looked earnestly into his eyes, "there is help for you! God has surely been talking to your heart and urging you to forsake your sins. Jesus at this very moment is holding out the life-line to you. The things that have just taken place seem severe and hard to bear, but it sometimes takes severe measures to awaken souls to their condition and danger. You are a great sinner in the sight of God. You have grieved and disobeyed Him, but He is merciful. It was for this very purpose that God sent His only Son into this evil world to suffer and die. It was not possible in God's plan of salvation for man to be saved without such a sacrifice. His Word tells us that whosoever believes that Jesus is the sacrifice for sin may be saved. Do you believe it?"

"Yes, Mother, with all my heart I believe it!" Byron answered.

"You must listen to the voice of God's Holy Spirit who has been talking to you of late," his mother continued. "The work of the Holy Spirit is to pilot you to the Father, where, with groanings that are too deep to be uttered, He will make intercession for you. In other words, the Holy Spirit will plead your case and will open your understanding so that you will see how to consecrate yourself to God. Then God, for His Son's sake, will pardon and redeem you, and you can live a life that will be worth living.

"But you will find that there is only one way to enter heaven, and that is by forsaking everything that is sinful and doing those things alone that will bring honor and glory to the Lord and His cause. You see, we are not our own. Jesus has bought us, and the price He paid was His own precious blood. When we have done all that our human abilities will enable us to do, we are still unprofitable servants. So it is not our goodness that takes us to heaven—though our deeds must be righteous—but it is through the goodness and mercy of God that we shall be able to enter heaven. When we have done all that is in our power to do, we are still debtors to God and to Christ; for Jesus paid our debt and blotted out the account against us, when He died upon the cross of Calvary.

"You may have had the idea, Byron, that the life of a Christian is a hard one, but this is not true. The Christian's life is the only life that is truly happy. It is the office of the Holy Spirit to make it so, for upon Him rests the responsibility of piloting us about among the rocks and through the storms of life. Life's journey is no imaginary voyage. All must take it, and the ocean is wide. How I wish that all would start out upon it fully prepared and see to it that they are aboard salvation's ship with the Holy Spirit as their Pilot.

"I believe that God has permitted these things to come upon you in order to help you to see your great need of the Savior. Jesus died for everyone in the world, and that includes you. God sees you now through His dear Son and wants to save you, and He will send His Holy Spirit into your heart. All you have to do is to be truly sorry for your sins and to be willing to do what He bids you. God will then do the work in your heart and will give you a right to the tree of life, that was forfeited by Adam and Eve."

Reaching for her Bible, she then turned to the twenty-first chapter of Revelation and read, " 'I am Alpha and Omega, the beginning and the end. I will give unto him that is athirst of the fountain of the water of life freely. He that overcometh shall inherit all things; and I will be his God, and he shall be my son. But the fearful, and unbelieving, and the abominable, and murderers, and whoremongers, and sorcerers, and idolaters, and all liars, shall have their part in the lake which burneth with fire and brimstone: which is the second death.'

"Byron, can't you see by this," she said, when she had finished reading, "how great God is and how eager He is to give eternal life to everyone who will ask for it, and how glad He is to accept them as His dear children?" Then she read, " 'Blessed are they that do his commandments, that they may have right to the tree of life, and may enter in through the gates into the city.'

"And," she continued, "further on we read that 'the Spirit and the bride'—the bride is God's church, or people—'say, Come. And let him that heareth say, Come. And let him that is athirst come. And whosoever will, let him take the water of life freely.'"

As the mother laid down her Bible, her older son came in from the barn, and the conversation was brought to a close.

"I know that you are both hungry," she said, rising to go into the dining room. "Come and eat your lunch. I prepared it early, but, not knowing when you would arrive, I've kept some of it warm."

Although the brothers had felt no desire for food since the night before, they were soon at the table and eating heartily. It seemed so good to have the great load of anxiety at last lifted. When the meal was ended, Byron slipped away to his room. Dropping wearily down upon his bed, he said to himself, "How could I ever have been so foolish? Why have I been so blind? Thank God that I can see at last how much Mother wants me to do well—and before I have utterly crushed her heart and life I can make amends!"

Sleep finally came to his relief. When he awoke, his mind and body were so rested that he was able to go into the field and spend several hours at hard work before supper time.

As he passed up and down between the long rows of corn, in the same field where he had once planted those beans, he though how he had been punished and admonished for his disobedience. He remembered how carefully he had tried to hide the beans, and he saw that the motive was the same as the one that had been leading him on with the boys. His evil deeds had developed and sprouted just as the beans did, and their growth had been just as rapid and surprising.

He saw not only the advantage of a pure, clean life, but the possibilities of attaining such a standard for himself. Jesus had really died for him, and God was willing and anxious to save him from a life of sin and to give him the Holy Spirit to guide him into all truth. He was anxious to make the start in this new life, but he felt that he must first endeavor to make his wrongs right, and he did not know where or how to begin.

When his brother returned the following day from the post office and laid the local newspaper down upon the table, Byron was not eager to read it as usual. A feeling of fear and shame swept over him. What if an account of his misdeeds was there? He was sure that if it was, they were pictured in glowing colors, and how could he look at it? He had often wondered how his name would look in print and had even wished that it might appear in the paper some time, but now he was really afraid that it was there.

When at last he could muster sufficient courage to do so, he slowly opened the paper and glanced hurriedly over the first page. He was surprised to find that there was nothing there about him and his companions; neither was there in the next few pages; and when he came to the last his fear had quite subsided. He was just about to decide that there was nothing in the paper about them when his eyes fell upon the glaring headlines that told the awful truth. Their arrest, their crimes, and their trial—all had been told to the public. He dropped the paper as if it been a coal of fire, and buried his face, burning with shame, in his hands.

What, oh, what would his friends say and think? How could he ever face them again? He felt that with this thing hanging over him he was disgraced forever.

With many thoughts of this nature in his mind, he tried to keep busy the remainder of the week. He longed to unravel the past, but it was in such a tangle that straightening it out would be no easy task. Many a time the miller's story came to his mind, and as he pondered upon it he was often reminded of his own duty. As the stolen tenth had grown and become troublesome to the miller, just so the results from the stealing of the eggs had increased on Byron's hands, and the wrong to his mother had spread to others. But his mother—dear, patient, faithful Mother—forgot that she had been wronged and did all in her power to help her penitent son out of his difficulties. She gladly gave her assistance, both in money and in making suggestions, until Byron could again look even Mr. Davis in the face with a clear conscience.

Some battles, however, Byron was forced to fight alone, for it is the only way that some conflicts can be rightly fought. For his own sake he needed some self-won victories, and they could come only through efforts that were put forth by himself.

The next Sunday morning Byron's mother was up bright and early as usual, preparing the breakfast for her family. As they came, one by one, into the kitchen where she was at work, she greeted them with a pleasant smile and a word of welcome; but when Byron came she kissed him and said, "Be sure, dear, not to be late for Sunday school. You know we must be there on time."

Her words confused Byron. He did not want to meet his teacher and much less the other members of his class, and for this reason he had decided not to attend church that day. "Mother," he said solemnly, "I have decided to remain at home today. I would like to be quiet and alone."

His mother understood the tone of his voice, but she quickly said, "O Byron, don't say that—you must go! I know it will be hard, but strive to be brave, and hasten with your work so that we shall not be late. You must meet your friends sooner or later, and the first meeting will be the hardest. Remember how very kind everyone has been to you so far."

So Byron was persuaded to go. But as they came in sight of the chapel, the fight within him increased and the struggle became fierce indeed. Several boys were in the churchyard standing near the hitching rack. Byron was well acquainted with all of them, and he knew that they must have either heard or read the piece in the newspaper. He would have been glad to avoid meeting these boys had it been possible to do so, and although they were looking at him, he did not speak to them as he passed on into the chapel to take his accustomed seat.

The service was especially good, but nothing impressed Byron so much as did the kindness of his teacher. Although she expressed no word or admonition on the subject of Byron's trouble, he knew that she had sympathy and he appreciated it with all his heart. The boys, too, tried to be kind, though they did not realize the change that had already taken place in Byron's heart. Byron did not have salvation, but he had found that there was no happiness in a life of sin. If only for his own comfort, he had decided to do right because it is right; but the other boys did not know this. Supposing that he was sorry only because his wicked deeds had been uncovered, they crowded around him as soon as the class was dismissed and began telling him how George and James were getting on in prison.

"They are having a fine time," one of them remarked. "Bob and I were at the county seat last week, and we made it a point to pay them a visit, and say, boys, listen to what they told us. They said that already they had learned to play several new games with cards, and no doubt they will catch on to a good many new tricks while they are there."

These words found no response in Byron's heart. He did not care to listen to them. James and George had passed out of his life, and he wanted to forget, if possible, all the evil that he had learned while in their company. Turning from the boys, he met his teacher's gaze and saw the troubled look in her face; but it instantly vanished as their eyes met, and an encouraging smile took its place. She, like his mother, seemed to understand something of his burden.

The sermon that day was unusually good. The minister, an elderly man, talked upon the perfect plan of salvation, and the thoughts he brought forth made deep impressions upon Byron's mind. As Byron had not been in the habit of paying close attention to the preaching, the old, old story of the creation seemed strangely new. He heard of God's great love for mankind after the fall, and of the day not far distant when the Lord will no longer invite men to accept His proffered love, but will judge them according to the way they have lived upon the earth, and he would have been glad to plead at once for the pardon of his sins. But Satan whispered, "Just wait a little while; you are not quite ready," and Byron listened.

As they rode home after the meeting, he was still sad, for the burden of his sins was resting heavily upon him; but his finer, better nature was aroused, and he drank in some of the beauties of nature. The bird songs made him glad, and their melody found an echo in his heart. The cornfields reminded him of husking time with its long hours of tedious toil. The chickens running along the roadside and the orchards made him think seriously. He wondered if Mr. Davis' young trees that George had cut would ever amount to anything, and if Jason would ever steal any more chickens from the tree near Mr. Sibley's home.

Passing an old farmhouse which was vacant and in which there was a window with a broken pane, Byron shuddered. His mother noticed and asked, "Are you cold, Byron?" but he replied, "No, I was only thinking." She said no more.

When they crossed the river bridge, the scene upon the foot log farther up the stream came once again to his mind. He could almost hear the gentle voice of the Holy Spirit warning him of danger, and he thought it strange that this voice had not been silenced, since he had so rudely cast the warnings aside. He was still being urged by the same patient, tender voice not only to change his course but to prepare himself for the journey of life.

CHAPTER X
THE LIFE-LINE

Byron had not yet discovered the wonderful life-line that had been cast to him by the loving hand of the Savior. He was still clinging, as it were, to a part of the wreckage of his past life, and his soul was in constant danger of being swept away either by the rising tide of discouragement or by the whirlwinds of temptation. God, by His Holy Spirit, was endeavoring to show him his only hope of safety and the things that had hindered him in his former efforts. But as yet he could not understand.

As they drove in through the gate, Byron drew a deep sigh of relief. It seemed so good to be at home again. Home was now to him a shelter from the tempestuous storms that were without—a haven and a place to rest. Mother understood. She asked no questions. They were not necessary. In morning worship, however, her prayers were a real source of comfort, for Byron realized that she was not talking into space with no one to hear. He knew too much now about that silent Listener—who is ever ready and waiting to carry a message either to God or to some loved one—not to understand in part the value of a mother's prayer.

During the week and the days that followed, Byron found plenty to occupy his time and thoughts. The farm work was very pressing; and as he toiled day after day in the field, his mind became filled with a new inspiration. He saw, as never before, his mother's responsibilities in caring for her family and discovered that it was not only his duty but his privilege to help her bear this burden. The thought seemed to arouse and cheer him, and his efforts became very noticeable and praiseworthy. But underneath this outward show he carried a burden which at times was almost unbearable and of which he could not rid himself.

One day while he was in a back field at work, the team needed a rest, so he climbed up as sat on the fence for a bit. With his jackknife he began whittling a small piece of wood, while the tired horses stamped and twitched at the flies that troubled them. Byron soon became buried in deep thought. His past life came before him as a book, and he read it page by page. He began with the early years of childhood, and the sweet memories thrilled him through and through. In those days his mother was all the world to him. He could go to her then with all his little troubles, and her word and kiss would brush them all away. As he read on in this imaginary book, he found that he had not maintained the same tender feeling and that a time came when he ceased to carry his troubles to mother. "But why should I," he reasoned. "I did not want to burden her unnecessarily."

Ah, that was not the reason. Reading on, he found that the voice of his conscience had often reproved him as a worthy pilot would a captain who was running his vessel into dangerous waters. His conscience had endeavored to pilot him in the right way, but his dear friend's counsel he had ruthlessly cast aside and to the gentle pleadings he had turned a deaf ear. He had not told his mother about his troubles, and her good advice given from time to time he had not heeded.

Some of the pages were full of trouble, and yet many had appeared as nothing to begin with, but which soon grew to be black, ugly mountains. He could now see how gently his mother had tried to lead him, how careful she had been lest some word of hers should cause him to think her harsh or unkind. He realized that he had misjudged her. The more he read, the more he could see that, although he had only continued along this path little by little, the results were certain. Each sin had led to a greater one.

He shuddered as he read the account of the stolen eggs. It was all there in black and white upon the pages of this memory book—the sudden flight of the hen, the burning sensation of the eggs upon his hand, his trip into the loft with them, his removal of the eggs; then to the grocer's remarks and the miller's story later on. Oh! why had he been so blind? Had he a right to a part of the produce that he had helped to raise? Yes, indeed, he had, but in no such way as that! He should have gotten his share with the rest and in an honorable way.

Little by little his wrongs came before him until he had reviewed his whole life. He now plainly saw that his recent trouble with the boys was only the outcome of his disobedience and the result of his smaller sins. He saw, too, that those sins had robbed him of his innocence and happiness, and that was why he was without rest or comfort.

He was a guilty sinner, lost on the ocean of sin. The wreck of his former self was stranded upon the mighty rock of Hope, but was liable to be swept away any moment by the waves of despair. He could see the Savior's lifeline, but it seemed so far away. He would have been glad to grasp it, but the effort seemed too great.

Poor Byron! He had endeavored to drown his feelings with hard work and had found it an impossibility. It could not be done! He felt that he was unable to raise himself out of his trouble by his own strength that unless he obtained salvation his life was ruined. The words, "Have mercy upon me, O Lord, for I am in trouble," flashed across his mind. His mother had read them in worship that very morning, but they had not appealed to him then as they did now.

Springing down from the fence, he quietly knelt down upon the soft ground and tried to pray. But all that he could do was to repeat the words of the psalm, which his mother had read. He was indeed in trouble, and he had never realized it so keenly as he did at that very moment. Oh, if only he had someone to whom he could unburden his heart!

In this state of mind he spent the remainder of the afternoon in the field, and when he returned to the house at the close of day, the load upon his heart had grown heavier, and his sufferings were almost greater than he could bear.

That evening he took a seat upon the porch as the golden streaks were fading away in the western sky. The scene before him was indeed beautiful, but he saw it not. He was looking away into the future and wondering what it held in store for him. "Oh, for the power to look beyond those hazy gates and read my own destiny," he sighed. Sitting thus in the twilight, with no definite purpose in view, he began to wish that something would happen to break the monotony of his thoughts, which were becoming almost unbearable. While he waited and thought, he heard a step behind him. Turning, he saw his mother approaching. She took the chair beside him.

She had noticed the sadness in her son's face from day to day, and as she saw it constantly deepening, she longed to see him happy and free again, as he used to be when a child. Realizing that nothing except full salvation could bring this to pass, she daily prayed for his conversion. Her mother heart was yearning to see him reach out and grasp the life-line that was being held out to him, before it was withdrawn, and ere he was swept away again into the billows of sin.

At first they talked only of the crops, the weather, and the probable harvest. Then a silence fell between them. It was one of those times which are so keenly felt because each, knowing the other's thoughts, waits for the other to break the silence.

"Byron," his mother finally said, "there is to be a series of meetings held in our neighborhood chapel, and they will begin next Sunday. A minister and some helpers and singers are to conduct the meetings. I am earnestly praying that God will grant us a profitable meeting. I feel sure it will be a source of help and inspiration to each one of God's children who will attend. And," she added, "I am praying that it may be a benefit to those who have not accepted Christ as their Savior, as well. I want to attend every service and should be pleased to have you to go with me."

The talk was continued long after darkness had covered the earth with its mantle and the stars were peeping out of the sky. There in the solitude of the night the confidence between mother and son, which had been broken, was restored. The mother found that her son was longing for that which she had been desiring him to possess, and her heart was cheered. The painful wound that she had received through his disobedience was instantly healed when she found how close the Savior had been to him that very day.

When Byron went to his room that night, he knelt beside his bed and tried to pray, but his words seemed to fall back upon his heart as lead. It seemed that he could think only of the coming meeting. And when he fell asleep, and he dreamed that he was in the chapel listening to a very touching sermon.

When Sunday came he was eager to go with his mother. It was for quite a different reason than he had once had. Before, he thought only of the boys and of the good times he expected to have in their company. Today he was eager to go in order to learn how to give his heart and life to God and become a whole-hearted Christian. Sinful pleasures and disobedient actions had lost all attraction to him, and he longed for the comfort of a conscience that was void of offense.

The meeting was in progress when Byron and his mother arrived, but the minister had not taken the pulpit. The company of workers consisted of one elderly woman, a middle-aged man, and three younger persons. As they sang, Byron noticed the happy expressions on their faces. They seemed to be singing from the depths of their hearts, and these were the words:

> Salvation's free, glad joy to all
>   Of Adam's fallen race;
> We'll tell to all, both far and near,
>   Of saving, keeping grace.

CHORUS: There's joy, glad joy,
>   Now flowing from above;
> There's joy, glad joy,
>   In the fullness of His love.

> From wells of everlasting joy,
>   Our strength by faith we bring;
> The joy that thrills my ransomed soul
>   Can make the dumb heart sing.

> How sweet the soul that's purged as pure
>   As gold without alloy!
> How peaceful is the flowing stream
>   Of deep, eternal joy!

> I'll live for Christ through this dark world,
>   And faithful I will be;
> The joy I know that keeps my soul
>   Shall last eternally.

How the words thrilled Byron's soul! That was the experience for which he was longing. Oh, to be able to draw joy from a well that would never run dry—what a privilege! How gladly he would live for Christ and be faithful if only he could have that joy that would last eternally.

When the song service was ended, someone said, "Let us pray." A number of the congregation knelt beside their seats, and Byron, although he only bowed his head, joined with them as best he could in prayer. After prayer another song was sung, and then the minister, stepping upon the rostrum, opened his Bible and began to preach about Christ's ministry upon the earth.

It was indeed a wonderful sermon. He recalled to the minds of the people the words of Jesus when He walked and talked in Galilee, and spoke of His simple life. He pictured the Savior's loving interest in mankind when He fed the hungry people and healed the sick. He rehearsed a part of the wonderful Sermon on the Mount, in which Jesus taught His disciples how to join Him in His work. He mentioned the great love of Christ when He stood at the grave of Lazarus and wept. Then he told of the Last Supper in the upper chamber. He related how, after Judas had passed out, Jesus spoke of the sad event that was about to take place and introduced the simple memorial of His death and gave a true emblem of humility by washing the disciples' feet.

Then, following the Savior across the brook Kedron, he led his hearers on into the lonely Garden of Gethsemane. There he showed them Jesus bowed in prayer, pleading to have the bitter cup taken from Him, if possible, but willing to drink its contents to the dregs, if necessary. Next he pointed out the clamoring mob, a short distance away, awaiting the Savior's approach, and the Roman soldiers grouped about the foot of the cross. The mangled Savior, pleading with the Father to forgive them, was a beautiful testimony of God's undying love.

The scene changed, and the congregation were allowed to look in ecstasy as he realized the full meaning of the empty tomb. He seemed to see the risen Lord seated on the throne beside His Father—the place which He occupied before His visit to the earth— and heard Him saying, "Come unto me, all ye that labour and are heavy laden, and I will give you rest. Take my yoke upon you, and learn of me; for I am meek and lowly in heart: and ye shall find rest unto your souls. For my yoke is easy, and my burden is light."

After the discourse there was singing and a few testimonies from the strangers, and Byron was more inspired than ever to make heaven his home. He became anxious to consecrate himself to the Lord, but as no opportunity was given, he returned to his home with the burden of sins still resting upon him.

The following day he could think of little else than the sermon and the happy faces of the strangers that he had looked upon in the chapel. As he thought, a picture of the ocean of life came before him. He could see the crafts floating about upon its surface, and he saw some of the rugged rocks upon which many of these vessels were wrecked. Some of these dangers were entirely hidden beneath the surface of the water, but each was shown on a chart with which all good seamen were familiar. On this chart there was a description of every hidden rock and a course mapped out whereby it could be avoided. Each obstruction that was visible bore a sign whereby its character might be discerned, but many of the signs were dimmed and blurred.

Some of the vessels that were floating carelessly about in the shallow waters, not heeding the instructions upon the chart, he saw torn to pieces and sunken. Others, although not so soon destroyed, were so battered and injured that they were unsafe.

On one of the flags that was floating above a forbidding rock, he saw the motto, "Do As I Please," and, to his amazement, he discovered, upon examining the chart, that more than half of the hidden dangers were located close around it. There was lying, stealing, hypocrisies, gambling, drunkenness, and many other rocks just beneath the surface of the water. Above another he read, "Worldly Pleasures," and around and about this he found such evils as he had not even dreamed could exist.

Many other things were pictured before him, but of all the sights in this great body of water, the one that interested him most was that of persons clinging to the parts of wreckage and floating about where the waters were deep and full of sharks and other dangers. Every moment he saw someone hurled down from a portion of a mast, a broken hull, or some other part of a wrecked vessel, to go down shrieking and groaning to his doom.

Byron shuddered as the scene passed before him, and he began looking out away from the shore. Here he discovered a promising ship with beautiful banners and streamers floating from it. Upon the banners he read, "Purity," "Honesty," "Kindness," "Holiness," and many other mottoes explaining the character of the passengers of the vessel.

The ship, too, he discovered, was not only strong and well-built, but traveled in a direct course and was out in mid-ocean. There it was in no danger of running into the snags which dotted the shallower water, for the water was much too deep for obstructions.

Now and then a lifeboat was lowered, and he saw that it was manned with the most competent sailors on board the ship. Watching them, he saw that although these life-saving crews went in among the snags and hidden rocks, they went only close enough to throw the life-line to those who were in distress. Those who did not realize their danger were simply warned, and the boat passed on to rescue those who were calling for help.

Looking back upon his own life, he saw that he had been stranded upon the hidden rocks near the obstruction "Do As I Please," and that he was now clinging to a very frail piece of wreckage. His danger was great, but the little company had come to his rescue in time and were throwing to him the life-line.

As he went to the meeting that night, he felt the burden of his sins more keenly than he had ever felt it before, and he was anxious to be rid of them. Night by night the plan of salvation was becoming more and more clear to him. He could see the two great kingdoms so strictly opposite and could discern the antagonism between them. He learned that in the beginning, man was heir to the kingdom of God, but that through lack of appreciation he lost his inheritance. He saw that when people reach the age of accountability, Satan, the cruel taskmaster, disguises himself and with enticing words and methods seeks to induce as many of them as possible to work for him. He saw, too, that it is only through the great love and mercy of God that it is possible for anyone to return, after forsaking the Lord to follow Satan.

He came to understand that heaven, so pure and holy in all its aspects, and so full of bright and happy beings, cannot contain one sinful atom; that man must become pure in heart in this world if he would enter those realms above. He perceived it was only love, infinite love and pity on the part of God, that had prompted Him to send Jesus to complete the plan of salvation, and that Jesus is the only door through which man can ever enter heaven or approach God.

The laws of Satan's kingdom, have, for a time, the appearance of liberty and freedom. But, as Byron had learned from experience, there is something which keeps the subjects of this kingdom from enjoying themselves for very long. On the other hand, he saw that the laws of heaven afford not only liberty but an inexhaustible supply of happiness as well.

Byron now wanted this liberty more than he had ever desired the freedom that the boys had suggested to him down by the river. He longed to be free so that he might do all he could in return for what Christ had suffered for him. And that he might also redeem his lost character, and, if possible, make his dear mother feel that her efforts to make him a respectable and honorable young man had not been in vain.

The sermon on repentance was deep and heart-searching, and the solemnity that rested upon the congregation was almost painful. When the minister ceased speaking a young man arose and urged the people to heed the words to which they had listened. He also gave them a kind and touching invitation to come forward for prayer. Then the company of workers joined in singing a beautiful song of invitation.

> Come home, poor sinner; Why longer roam,
> Thy Savior's calling, "Come home, come home!"

CHORUS

> Jesus is pleading; He's interceding;
> Yes, pleading, pleading
> For thee to come;
> Come home, poor sinner, Come home, come home.

> He died to save you, On Calvary;
> Behold what suff'ring! 'Twas all for thee.

> Oh, come to Jesus, Do not delay;
> Come, and He'll save you; Come while you may.

> Oh, come to Jesus; He's waiting still

With His salvation, Thy soul to fill.

Oh, come to Jesus; How can you stay,
He's pleading, pleading; Come, come today.

Byron was glad for such an opportunity. With his poor, aching heart painfully throbbing in his bosom, he hastened to the front, and there with several others humbled himself in prayer. The minister bowed beside him and explained in a simple manner what it really means to repent and to be truly saved from a sinful life.

"My dear young man," he said, "you have acknowledged to your friends, by the simple act of humbling yourself in prayer, that you intend to live a new and different life. But you cannot do this in your own strength. God alone can save you and He can help you meet the conditions laid down in His Word. He says, first of all, to repent, and this means to be sorry for all the sins that you have committed.

"Now, there is a kind of sorrow that comes from having your wicked deeds found out, but this is not true repentance. To have godly sorrow is to be troubled and pained because one has violated God's holy law, brought dishonor to His character and government, and shown ingratitude toward His infinite love and benevolence.

"John the Baptist went about preaching repentance, and Jesus a few years later re-echoed the message of God's commandment to mankind; the commandment was not given to only a few individuals, but to everyone."

Turning to his Bible, the minister read Acts 17:30, and then said, "When a person has become truly sorry for his sins he is to call upon God for help, for in Isaiah we read that we are to seek the Lord while He may be found.

"There are, of course, conditions to be met in repentance. When you have become truly sorry for having offended your Creator, you must seek for His pardon. He will be close to you when He sees your sorrow, and you must call upon Him to help you."

Again he read from his Bible: " 'Seek ye the Lord while he may be found, call ye upon him while he is near.' By this you see that you not only must 'call' upon God to save you, but must actually seek

His favor. See, this next verse will show you how: 'Let the wicked forsake his way, and the unrighteous man his thoughts: and let him return unto the Lord, and he will have mercy upon him; and to our God, for he will abundantly pardon.'

"To forsake your way is to turn from every evil motive that has prompted you in the past to commit sin and to utterly abandon your old life of sin. You must make an unconditional surrender to God. You must not only acknowledge your sins to Him, but be willing to have them all exposed if necessary.

"Now God commands you to repent. There is no other way. If you want salvation, you must get it according to the rules laid down in the Bible. There are many other scriptures bearing upon this subject. God says, 'To day if ye will hear his voice, harden not your heart.'" (Byron thought at once of the voice that had spoken to him down by the river.) "You can apply this promise to yourself, for now is the time for you to hear His voice and to accept His salvation. Here is another: 'Behold, now is the accepted time; behold, now is the day of salvation.' God wants you to yield yourself to Him, right now, to live the remainder of your life for Him and for His glory.

"Do you willingly promise that you will do anything that God may require of you? He will not tell us to do something impossible. He simply asks you to be willing and ready to make your wrongs right wherever you can. This is but just and right, and is one of the fruits worthy of repentance that is spoken of in Luke 3:8, and also in Acts 26:20. 'He that covereth his sins shall not prosper: but whoso confesseth and forsaketh them shall have mercy.'

"Then, too, you must not only be willing to confess your sins and ask forgiveness for them, but forgive all who have wronged you in any way, for 'if ye forgive not men their trespasses, neither will your Father forgive your trespasses.'"

"All of these things I have done," Byron said in a low voice when the minister ceased speaking. "I have confessed to God and have gone to those whom I have wronged and have made things right as well as I could. What more can I do?"

"There is still another step," the minister said very earnestly. "You are well on the way, but you still have a great barrier to remove. Unbelief and disobedience have severed you from God, and you can only win favor with Him again by replacing these with obedience and belief in the gospel. The Bible does not say to 'believe the gospel and repent,' but to 'repent... and believe the gospel,' and what is meant by the gospel is found in John 3:16: 'For God so loved the world, that he gave his only begotten Son, that whosoever believeth in him should not perish, but have everlasting life.' Can you not see God's love and mercy? Can you not believe that the great sacrifice that He made for sin is for you, too?

"You are changing masters. The power of Satan is broken. You are no longer his servant, but are instead to be subject to a higher, nobler Power than his, if you will but believe. And God is waiting to give you His Holy Spirit to direct and pilot you in all of your undertakings, after you have discovered the secret of believing."

"I do believe," Byron said a moment later, and the tone of his voice and expression of his face showed plainly that a change had taken place. He had indeed discovered the secret of salvation. Arising to his feet, he faced the congregation, and in a voice that was clear and distinct and a manner that was happy and free, he spoke of the new life that he expected to live before them in the future. "My dear friends and companions," he said, "I want to tell you that I have decided to change my course in life. The rest of my days shall be spent in the Lord's service. I am truly sorry for all that I have ever done to displease Him."

Byron seemed already to feel a deep joy and satisfaction in the fact that he had made his peace with God and was able to claim an heirship with the Savior. So confident were his words that his old associates looked upon him with awe, and some felt in their hearts a desire to share his happiness.

Chapter XII
Anticipations of the Journey

That evening, after bidding his mother good night, Byron hastened to his room. There, alone in the quiet of the night, he bowed beside his bed and breathed a prayer of thanksgiving to God for His great love and compassion. For a moment his past life again came before him, with all of its sinfulness and blunders pictured in glowing colors, but it instantly vanished, and his heart leaped with joy, for he knew that his old life was all gone forever.

A picture of the future, made beautiful because of the presence of the Savior and a life of usefulness for himself, floated before him. He could see his pathway, leading ever upward in his Christian career, at last disappearing in the glories of the life to come, and as he laid his head upon his pillow, angels seemed to be comforting him.

When the worship hour arrived in the morning, Byron took the Bible that was handed him by his mother, and as he read from its pages the words seemed strangely new and interesting to him. When he went out to work in the field, he was still thinking of what he had read. "A day in thy courts is better than a thousand. I had rather be a doorkeeper in the house of my God, than to dwell in the tents of wickedness. For the Lord God is a sun and shield: the Lord will give grace and glory: no good thing will he withhold from them that walk uprightly. O Lord of hosts, blessed is the man that trusteth in thee." These words had been memorized at Sunday school, but never before had they appealed to him as they did upon that particular morning.

He was certainly enjoying more true happiness out there in the field alone with nature and his God than he had ever been able to imagine before. He felt that it would indeed be an honor to be able to fill the very lowest place in the house of God. So happy was he as he worked that he seemed to be living in a new world. And while the merry songsters appeared to be warbling their sweetest anthems for his special benefit, he joined with them, as had been his habit in childhood, before his innocence had fled.

He realized that Christ the Savior had wrought the change, and he knew that he was not enjoying such happiness alone. His precious mother no longer bore the careworn expression that she had endeavored to conceal by a smile when anyone was around. She, too, was answering the little birds with a song of gladness.

Byron was now prepared for his ocean voyage. His former experience had taught him that he could rely upon the advice of the Holy Spirit, for no one understood God's chart, the Bible, better than this faithful Pilot.

The meetings continued for several weeks, and many souls were enlightened, and some, like Byron, found deliverance from a life of sin. Among the number were some of Byron's associates before he met with James, and he rejoiced that he could still have them for his friends and companions.

When the morning service of the last day's meeting was just about to close, the minister announced that in the afternoon there would be baptismal services at the river. At the appointed time the river's banks on either side were thronged with people who desired to witness the solemn scene. The little group of Christians from the chapel passed down to the water's edge, and there, beneath the overhanging branches of the trees, they offered a short prayer to God. When they arose, their voices filled the air with strains of heavenly music, and one of the scenes of the long ago was repeated. Slowly the minister and one of the candidates passed out into the stream as a sweet hymn floated upward.

> Down into the flowing river,
>   Lo, the lamb of God we see;
> There He speaks in clear example:
>   "Take the cross and follow Me."
>
> Gently buried with my Savior,
>   Let me sink beneath the wave;
> Crucified to earth forever,
>   Hence alone to God I live.
>
> Now the sacred waters cover
>   O'er the holy Son of God;
> Thus He washed me in that fountain
>   Of His sin-atoning blood.

> Crucified with my Redeemer,
> Now I sink into the grave;
> I am dead to sin forever,
> By the life of God I live.
>
> Here I witness a confession
> As I merge from human sight,
> In the tomb of yielding water,
> That the blood has made me white.
>
> Oh, how sweet to follow Jesus,
> In this ordinance to show
> That we're cleansed in life's pure river,
> Even whiter than the snow.

One by one the candidates followed their Savior's example and were buried in a watery grave, thus testifying to the world that they were dead to sin; by representing the death, burial, and resurrection of Jesus, they were buried unto His death.

Byron was among the number. As he entered the water, there was a peaceful smile upon his face. He was thinking of the scene where John the Baptist was baptizing the people in the river Jordan, and he imagined that he could see the lovely form of Jesus just entering the water as he was now doing. He could see, in the picture, the troubled expression upon the face of the brave prophet and hear him humbly saying, "I have need to be baptized of thee, and comest thou to me?" and then Jesus answering, "Suffer it to be so now: for thus it becometh us to fulfil all righteousness."

In fancy Byron saw the Savior buried in Jordan's waters, and a moment later arise again; then the heavens opened and the Holy Ghost descending from above. He also seemed to hear the Father saying, "This is my beloved Son, in whom I am well pleased."

How different this scene from the one that a short time before had presented itself to Byron while the Holy Spirit talked to him upon the foot log. He thanked God that he had heard the voice and had heeded the warning in time to escape destruction. As he sank into the watery grave himself, he felt that sweet consolation that is the result of having fulfilled every known duty, and the assurance that his heavenly Father accepted him as His own dear son. There was no loud voice to utter the words, "I am well pleased," but the Holy Spirit whispered them in his heart.

Many regretted that the evening's service would be the last and that the little group whom they had learned to love must leave in the morning, but they were glad that so many had found deliverance from the bondage of sin.

As the minister bade Byron farewell, he remarked, "God surely has His hand upon you for service. Be faithful when He calls you into His work. There are many souls who are being tossed about upon the billows of sin, as you were. They are calling for help from far and near. Be ready when you hear their pleading, and haste to their rescue. God bless you and make you a power in His hands."

As Byron began his various duties upon the farm the following day, his highest ambition was to do with his might what his hands found to do and to perform it cheerfully as unto the Lord. From a few words that his mother had said at the breakfast table he had learned a beautiful secret. "In our efforts to please God," she had said, "we cannot please Him perfectly unless we willingly and cheerfully do the little trying things that daily fall to our lot. When we have properly performed these, He trusts us with greater responsibilities, for we are then more able to bear them. It is like testing a vessel in which we desire to put liquid. We pour in just a little to test it before we trust it with the full amount."

Byron wanted to bear the tests. He desired to be very useful for the Lord. Often, while his team was resting, he would steal away to some secluded spot and there pour out his heart in prayer to God. At times he was assailed by the enemy, but under such tests he went to his mother and there found the help and advice that he needed. Her suggestions were so to the point and he was so much in earnest that he advanced rapidly in his Christian life and duties.

He no longer dreaded family worship, but, on the contrary, enjoyed taking an active part in it. His mother proposed many things that made it very interesting. Sometimes they would endeavor to find the most important thought contained in the chapter read and would meditate upon it through the day; sometimes they would take some Bible character and compare his or her life with some modern person whom they knew; sometimes each member of the family would choose some verse in the Bible, and they would read and discuss these, endeavoring to draw from them every good point that they possibly could. In this way God's Word became real to Byron and was daily food to his soul.

Byron had found the source of true happiness. He had found, too, that there were two days that never caused him trouble any more. One of these days was yesterday. Yesterday was gone! Whatever had occurred on that day he could never undo. Not one word could he recall. All of its pains, sorrows, and regrets were forever sealed and far beyond his reach. He was glad for this. He was glad that the storm clouds that had thickened but a few yesterdays ago could never sweep over him again. The past could never return. It belonged to God.

The other day was tomorrow. Tomorrow was also far beyond his reach. No human effort could bring it closer. Its burdens, its sorrows, its perils, its mistakes and blunders, were as yet a mystery and sealed. The sun might shine in all its splendor or be hidden by weeping clouds, but the day belonged to God. Tomorrow would appear, it must appear as long as time continued; but when it came it would no longer be tomorrow, but today.

Byron's only day, then, was today. What he accomplished must be done on that day, for how could he know whether he would be alive when the next arrived. So he decided that he could and would be faithful in all that was committed to his charge. And he thought with great relief that he could fearlessly leave his yesterdays and his tomorrows in the care of his all-wise Creator.

It was well for Byron that his days had thus been committed to God, for on one occasion he was permitted to have a glimpse of the future with all its varied possibilities. A relative from a distance, who was a Christian man, came to the farm for a week's visit. During his stay he became greatly interested in Byron's faithfulness in performing his various Christian duties. Several times he went with Byron to the field and there, as they worked side by side, Byron's character and principles were displayed to the other's satisfaction.

One evening, shortly before he was to leave, this man was talking with Byron's mother about the great change in her son's life and conduct. He surprised her by saying, "I don't know what you will say when I tell you of what I have been thinking, but when I have made my proposition you may consider it or not as you wish. Now, I realize your care and anxiety concerning Byron's future, and how hard it will be for you to part with him, but I should like to have him return with me to my home and enter my place of business. What do you say to his going?"

So sudden was the thought of parting with her son that for a few minutes the mother was speechless, and in spite of her efforts to be calm, the tears began to trickle down her cheeks.

Realizing the depth of her feelings, the relative continued, "I do not wonder at your sorrow, but I do not think that you will ever regret the sacrifice if you will permit him to go. Byron is a bright young man, and his possibilities are great. I feel a deep interest in him, and I not only will help him to develop into a good businessman, but will see that he has opportunity to grow spiritually as well. I know that you will miss him here in the home and upon the farm, but I believe that his younger brother will soon be able to take his place in the work, and your heart will be comforted by the thought that your boy is where his mind and character can broaden out in God's service. The noble traits of character you have faithfully tried to instill within him will then be shown, and I promise to be to him all that anyone except his own mother can be."

It was some time before the mother could speak, but at last she said, "It is certainly hard to give him up, but, as you say, it may be the best to let him go. Byron has had some talks with me concerning his future course in life, and I have been at a loss just how to advise him. I believe that what you suggested will be just what he has been aspiring to, although of late he has said nothing about it. But here he is coming now. Let us talk the matter over with him."

When Byron entered the room, he could not understand why his mother and the visitor looked so solemn. But when he was told why, his countenance instantly brightened, and when asked what he thought of the plan, he said with excitement, "Oh, I'm sure I should like to go! But," he added, looking into his mother's tear-stained face, "I don't see how I could go. Mother needs me here at home. The work on the farm has increased in the past two years so much that I could not be spared, and then," with a little break in his voice, "I'm afraid that you will—or might—I mean—perhaps—" Poor Byron! He could not say what he desired to say, but his mother helped him out.

"You mean, Byron, that you are afraid that I could not give up my boy?" she asked.

"Yes, Mother, it was that. I was thinking how hard it would be to part with you, and I know that a mother's love is much deeper than her child's."

The love which that mother's eyes spoke could not be described—so deep yet so submissive and firm.

"Yes, my boy, I am willing for you to go," she replied. "It will, of course, be very hard to give you up, but there is no blessing without some degree of sacrifice, and I am glad to commit you to the care of one whom I believe is more able to help you now than myself. With the Holy Spirit as your guide and this good man as your friend and counselor, you should be able to develop into a useful Christian man and be a blessing to the world. I shall be comforted with knowing that, though you are far away, you will be able to write and tell me how you are doing, and can also come to me sometimes."

CHAPTER XIII
THE PILOT'S WORK

That evening Byron was alone with his mother in her room. To leave his home was hard, but to part from the one who had been so loving and patient with him even in disgrace was harder still. Through his past failures he had discovered his own weakness and shortcomings, and had learned the true value of his mother's counsel.

"Tell me, Mother," he said, when they were comfortably seated, "all that will be helpful to me in times of trial and temptation. I want to be all that God wants me to be, but you know I might be tempted to do wrong; if you do not point out dangers, I may unconsciously make mistakes by not understanding the instructions of the Holy Spirit."

"My son, you are right," his mother replied. "The young must be warned of danger and taught to avoid the snares that are laid for their feet. There is one danger of which I have told you, but now that you are about to leave me and make new acquaintances in other places, I should like to impress the warning more deeply, if possible, upon your mind.

"Byron, the drunkard is not made in a moment. Neither is the young man liable to fall dead from the effect of his first drink, although the first drink may be his downfall. He must shun the first drink if he would escape the second.

"Some people are born with an unnatural appetite and desire for liquor that makes it hard for them to resist temptation. Others have the weakness of character and willpower that makes them unable to bear the ridicule and threats of their comrades, as you found in your association with James. Such people are to be pitied and taught the results of yielding to temptation."

"Mother," Byron said thoughtfully as she paused, "I don't think I've told you about a certain experience I had last summer. For truly I was ashamed to tell you. I knew you ought to know it, but I did not feel then as I do now. It is really a relief to tell you now about my troubles, for you encourage me so much.

"Do you remember the time when I was sent to Mr. E——'s to help in the harvest field? Well, it was an extremely hot day, and the men, working so hard at picking up the bundles of grain, got very thirsty. One of the boys was kept busy carrying water to us.

"About the middle of the afternoon Mr. E—— himself took the water pail and left for the house and when he returned I noticed that he held a dipper in one hand. Some of the men that were near gathered about him, and from their merry mood I decided that the farmer must be telling them some very interesting story.

"I quickly dropped the bundle I was holding, and joined them. But as I came near they all became strangely silent. In a moment, however, they began speaking in low tones to one another, and by their winks and glances in my direction I decided they must be talking about me. Being very thirsty, I did not wait to investigate, but reached for the dipper and was just about to dip it into the pail when I discovered that the pail did not contain water.

" 'Oh, take a drink, Byron,' one of the men said when he saw me hesitate. 'Here is something that will quench your thirst all right.'

"I said that I wanted something that would. I was just about to take a drink, but hesitated again and said, 'Mr. E——, what is this, anyway? I like to know what I'm drinking.'

" 'Oh, it's just something to brace you up and strengthen you for hard toil and keep you from drinking so much water,' he answered.

"So I tasted what was in the dipper. It was not what I was expecting, and I did not like it; but when one of the men said, 'It is only a little cider,' I took another swallow.

" 'Cider? Why, I have never tasted cider like this, and how is it that they can have cider at this time of year?'

" 'You see, Byron,' said Mr. E——, 'this is some that I kept over from last year, and it is just a little aged, but it will do the work, all right. All the other fellows here are drinking it, and say it's fine.'

" 'Well, if it's all right as you say, I will try to drink some more,' I told him, 'for I don't like to drink so much water.'

"So I tried it again. This time I drank several swallows, and in a short time I took a little more.

"Not long after I had taken the second drink, I began to feel queer and dizzy. When I would reach for a sheaf, it would suddenly come toward me. The men noticed my condition and began to laugh and make sport of me. Finally I had to stop work altogether and go and lie down in the shade.

"Now, Mother, I had heard that hard cider contained alcohol, but I had no idea that it was really hard cider that I was drinking or that its effect upon the system would be so rapid.

"I did not feel any better after I had lain down, and it was some time before I could go back to work in the field. Later, one of the men explained that my bad feelings came from the alcohol in the cider. I was so ashamed of it all that I decided not to tell you if possible, and here I have told you all about it myself. I am sure of one thing, however, and that is that no one can ever get me to drink hard cider again."

"Your experience is like that of many a boy, Byron," his mother remarked. "Unwarned of the dangers that are in the world, many are caught unaware in the traps that are laid for their feet. I see that I have been a little tardy in warning you of some things, but I rejoice to know that the cider did you no greater harm.

"But strong drink is the undoing of many a life. Some time ago I found and marked a few scriptures on this subject in my Bible, and I want to read them to you now.

" 'Who hath woe? Who hath sorrow? Who hath contentions? Who hath babblings? Who hath wounds without cause? Who hath redness of the eyes? They that tarry long at the wine; they that go to seek mixed wine. Look not thou upon the wine when it is red, when it giveth his color in the cup, when it moveth itself aright. At the last it biteth like a serpent, and stingeth like an adder.'

" 'Woe unto them that rise up early in the morning, that they may follow strong drink; that continue until night, till wine inflame them!'

" 'Woe unto him that giveth his neighbor drink.'

"And 'be ye not unwise, but understanding what the will of God is. And be not drunk with wine, wherein is excess; but be filled with the Spirit.'

"Wines that intoxicate and ruin both soul and body of mankind should be let alone.

"And, Byron, there is another thing I wish to speak to you about before you leave me. It is the choosing of your friends. You have had some experience of this nature, but I believe you still need advice.

"In the choice of your friends do not be hasty. Be sure that the one whom you take for a friend is an excellent person in every sense of the word. You may wonder how you can know, for human nature is so deceptive. You may perhaps be deceived by some, and you will find that all have their own peculiar faults; but this need not discourage you. There are many who are worthy and whose company you will enjoy, and through your association with them you will receive a lasting benefit.

"Never choose a friend beneath yourself except when you see in him virtues that need to be brought to the surface, and you can be a help to him. Never sink to such a person's level, but strive to bring him up to yours. When you find that this cannot be done, drop him at once. In helping another without yielding to his influence, you make advancement yourself, for every good deed will move you forward and upward.

"Through an encouraging word spoken at the proper time many have not only won a lifetime friend, but have helped someone to overcome a difficulty that might have utterly discouraged him. Let 'Kindness and Duty' be your motto, Byron, and strive to make friends of those in whom you see virtue and honor. Have a purpose in all that you do and thus build up your spiritual character.

"Remember that you are in God's ship now, ready to do service for your Master and King. You may sometimes go out upon a life-saving expedition and throw the life-line to the lost, but you cannot help them unless they will grasp and hold firmly to the line. Your Pilot will guide you to those who are worthy if you will listen to His voice, and by helping them you may find a true and lasting friend."

It was hard to find a stopping place in the conversation, but at last

Byron bade his mother good night. As his lips touched her brow, he smoothed back the locks above it with his hand and whispered, "God bless you, Mother, I will strive to put into practice what you have told me, and listen for my Pilot's voice.

Byron was extremely busy during the next few days. There was a trip to town for a new suit, shoes, and other things needed, and then all of his belongings had to be carefully gone over to see that nothing was missed that would be useful to him. Mother cleaned, brushed, washed, mended, and ironed until the last article was ready to be packed.

When all was in readiness and the day of his departure had arrived, he again slipped away to his mother's room. He found her waiting for him with her Bible in her hand, for she was expecting him. She had something more to tell him.

"Byron, my boy," she tenderly said, drawing his chair closer to her own, "there are a few more things I wish to speak about before you leave me.

"When you go away, I trust that you will remember the times we have spent together in this room. I shall often bow here again in prayer for you, as I have done in the past, for I well know you will have many new and strange trials to meet. You cannot expect to go through the world and escape them. They are inevitable. But there will be something about every trial that you may have that will increase your understanding of God's will concerning you and will make you stronger and wiser for those that follow. Remember, dear, that nothing can separate you from God except transgression and disobedience. God will carry you through every difficulty if only you will allow Him to do so.

"I hope you will improve every opportunity for gaining knowledge that will be useful and helpful to you in later years. I believe you understand now why it is necessary to keep company with good people if you would do right, but there are other companions with whom you can associate and receive even greater harm than from sinful persons.

"Bad literature, I believe, is the worst comrade that one can have. In your short association with James you discovered some of the effects of novel reading, for you have told me how it inspired you to be bold and daring and anxious to perform evil deeds. Well, there is a type of reading that is scarcely better than this and that many read, but its effect upon the mind and character it is quite as harmful. It is found in books that have been written simply to entertain and amuse, and not in any way to improve the reader. Such books may be termed trash and compared to things to eat that have taste good, but contain hardly any nourishment. A child fed upon such things could not develop properly, but would become dwarfed and be unable to accomplish much of anything. Just so it is with those who feed their minds with unwholesome literature.

"You may be sure that Satan does not allow an opportunity of that kind to escape his notice. With all of his alluring powers he seeks to draw such an individual away from God. The old adage that 'Satan finds mischief for idle hands to do' is just as true of idle minds. Little by little, readers of trashy literature fall into a careless, haphazard way of thinking and are unable to concentrate their thoughts long enough to gain a benefit from wholesome reading when they try.

"But books that contain the biographies of good men and travels narrated in a sensible way will not have this tendency and are safe to read, and I wish that you would read some books of this character. Reading about good men will be helpful in drawing out your own better qualities. And books on nature, astronomy, history, etc., are mostly good. By reading them you will gain a wider, broader knowledge of the earth and the people who live upon it. Classical reading, too, will be helpful in elevating your mind and ideals.

"I want you to improve every opportunity that you can to gain knowledge that will be helpful to you, but above all things else do not neglect your Bible. Read it often and read it carefully. Let it be your daily food. Nothing will be more uplifting to your principles. It is indeed a library in itself and is acknowledged by the best authorities to be the choicest and most important collection of books in our literature. It enlightens the mind and satisfies the soul. It makes impossibilities possible, and its words and teaching are eternal. And, best of all, it will give to all who read it a purpose in life worth striving for.

"Byron, those who have a purpose in life do not need a set of rules governing what they shall and shall not do. They will not be asking,

'Do you think I could do this or that and keep saved and out of trouble?' Their thought will be, 'Can I do this to the glory of God and the advancement of His cause, or will it injure my influence among those whom I wish to help?' They may go to someone for counsel; but if they receive an explanation showing that the thing in question would prove a hindrance to themselves and others, they will not complain, or think themselves martyrs without any freedom. God wants His people to be examples of His kingdom. And it is for the purpose of guiding them aright that He has sent His Holy Spirit into the world. One duty of this Pilot is to warn Christians of danger by bringing to their mind the many snares that the enemy has prepared to entrap them, and to teach them by the aid of His chart, the Bible, how to avoid them.

"It is true that God's people are in the world and must in many ways live just as worldly people do. They must eat, drink, sleep, and go about their daily toil; but in their actions and desires they are different from worldly people. They desire to please their heavenly Father in everything they do, and they do not consider such service a hardship or a burden.

"It takes only a very tiny sin to stain the soul. So, Byron, if you would be a child of God, have your heart and life set against everything that is evil.

"And now, my son, a word about your Christian duty, and I think you will be quite well prepared to leave me. Do not neglect your Christian obligations, Byron. Remember that there are responsibilities placed upon each person that can be performed only by them. If you shirk responsibility because you think yourself unqualified for the task, remember that your heavenly Father will correct you as an earthly parent does a disobedient child. If God does not want to use you, He will not burden you for service."

"Well, then, Mother, why is it," Byron asked in a perplexed manner, "that some people have been mistaken in regard to their calling and have found that they did not understand what the Lord really wanted them to do? I have heard several testify in prayer meeting that they had been mistaken as to their calling."

"It was because they failed to consult with the Holy Spirit and did not wait until they knew what the Lord really wanted them to do," his mother answered. "You see, everyone has his own ideas of service, and some seek promotion, while others care more for a humble place. Those like the ones you mentioned act upon their own desires, instead of tarrying until God gives them a special line of work; in other words, they use their own judgment in the matter. If you are not hasty, God will make the course that He wishes you to pursue very plain, and with the Holy Spirit to pilot you, there is no reason for you to make mistakes.

"Now, if your calling is a desirable one, Satan may attempt to make you think highly of yourself. But remember this: when you have done all that in your power lies for the good of the cause; when you have sacrificed your friends, home, and all that human ties hold dear; when you have suffered affliction and sorrows, you still are an unprofitable servant. You never can erase by human effort the blot of sin, nor pay the debt of the world. God's sacrifice was so great that none of us can ever cease to be under obligations to Him, and we should rejoice that it is our privilege to serve One so worthy and gracious. Byron, you are now a servant, but a servant of the most noble and glorious King that ever sat upon a throne."

Chapter XIV
The Life-Preserver

The hour of departure had at last arrived. The carriage stood in front of the house, and the valises and suitcases carefully loaded. It was a few hours before train time, but as the station was several miles distant, it was thought best to start in good season.

As the family gathered about Byron and one by one grasped his hand to bid him goodbye, it was with difficulty that he managed to keep back the tears. Mother came last. Unable to control himself any longer, he threw himself into her arms and wept. The pent-up fountain of tears gushed forth as rain, but the cloud burst lasted only for a moment. Whispering, "Dear Mother, goodbye," he kissed her tenderly and stepped into the carriage.

The evening shadows stretched long as they turned onto the highway. Byron looked back and saw his mother standing near the gate. Instantly two other scenes flashed before his mind. In one he had left without his mother's consent and in the other with a broken heart because of his transgression. Now he was leaving the same gateway with a mother's benediction and approval resting upon him. Then he had been miserable, full of guilt and condemnation, but now he was free and happy in the assurance that he was doing right and that God's Spirit was leading him. What a change! And in so short a time! Byron could hardly realize it himself. Truly he was a new creature. Old things had passed away, and the world appealed to him differently. He now had not only a Pilot to guide and direct him according to God's chart, the Bible, but a life-preserver as well. The latter had been discovered in the atoning blood of Jesus after his heart had been cleansed and made pure and white.

As Byron rode on toward the station, his thoughts were continually returning to his home and mother. Nothing could ever erase the memory of the happy times that he had spent upon the farm and around the home fireside. Now and then little glimpses of summertime games and of wintertime frolics flashed before him. They were all over now. Never again could he expect to mingle his voice in those boyish sports. They were past. He might return, but everything would be different. Sometimes he might again crack nuts in the dining room on the stones about the open fireplace and pop corn upon the kitchen range; but his siblings, like himself, would be older and changed. Was he, down deep in his heart, glad for the change?

As he thought of the expression upon his mother's face when she waved him farewell from the gate, he was both glad and sorry. He was glad that he was going away with his mother's approval resting upon him, and sorry because he was leaving the home that had sheltered him from both the literal and the spiritual storms of life.

Realizing suddenly that he had been meditating upon his yesterdays, which were forever sealed to him, he turned his thoughts into the future with all its possibilities of both failure and success. Would he have success in his business life, or would his efforts toward success be a failure? He seemed to hear his mother saying as she had so often remarked, "What is worth doing at all, Byron, is worth doing well," and he instantly decided to accept these words as his motto in his business career and to leave his tomorrows to the care of his Pilot.

The train was late. While they were waiting, Byron's companion said, "I hope, Byron, that you will not regret the step you are taking and that you will like your new home and surroundings when we reach our destination. A sudden change from the freedom of the country is sometimes hard to get used to by young folks when they first enter the city. I have no doubt that things will be strangely different to you, but I trust that, as you throw yourself into your new line of work, you will like it.

"Success does not come in a moment, and those who would attain to it need an abundant supply of courage and determination, and a decision to make the best of everything. It will be necessary for you to be on your guard and watchful for both advantages and temptations."

"I am determined," Byron answered, "to put forth every effort to succeed. Others whose opportunities were far beneath mine have succeeded, and I believe that I may if I will."

"Yes, Byron, you may succeed financially," his companion replied, "but I want to see you reaching out in another direction as well. Never forget your mother's teachings and warnings. Be ever on your guard, for the enemy is very sly and cunning. He is roaming the earth seeking unwary souls as his prey. It will be necessary for you to diligently read and pray and then to apply the various scriptures that you find in your Bible to yourself. Never think that because someone else who is professing is doing a certain way, it is proper and right for all of God's children to follow that person's example.

"Upon such occasions listen for the voice of your Pilot, heed His warnings, and be sure that you obey the orders that He gives you. It is best to refer often to the chart and see that the orders agree perfectly with the chart's directions and to know that you thoroughly understand them. But never cast any orders carelessly aside, considering them of no profit to you. The warnings of the Holy Spirit are very necessary and valuable, but God wants you to prove all spirits by the Bible, and to know that it is really the Holy Spirit that is talking to you, for there are many spirits in the world waiting to deceive the Christian. Their highest aim and endeavor is to cause a soul to lose its way. Beware of such spirits, Byron. They are false and will not agree with God's Word.

"There may be some terrific storms, but remember, though the

Thunder rolls and storm clouds fall,
God's loving hand is in it all,

and that His grace is sufficient to keep you."

Byron was truly thankful for his friend's advice and interest in him, though it was many years before he realized how needful it had been.

The delayed train at last drew up to the station, and a few minutes later Byron and his friend were speeding toward their distant home. After a long and tiresome journey they arrived at their destination. As Byron stepped from the train, he felt himself in a strange land.

His simple life upon the farm had given him a very limited knowledge of the world, but he soon became adjusted to his new surroundings and applied himself diligently to every new duty. As the days and weeks sped by, his faithful efforts to perform each task properly were very noticeable, and he was often promoted to a more responsible place.

Realizing he needed of a better education, Byron spent much of his spare time studying, especially his Bible. While alone in his room, in the stillness of evening, he often recalled his mother's comforting words and advice, and they always seemed to strengthen him to press on toward success.

One evening as he sat by the window in deep meditation, his thoughts wandered back to the old home and farm. It was an ideal summer evening, and in fancy he could see his mother and all of the dear ones scattered about in the yard and upon the porch, and could hear the merry laughter of his younger brother with his playmates upon the lawn. As memories one by one crowded in upon his mind, he felt a great sense of loneliness stealing over him. He longed for those hours of pleasure once more, but they were gone. He wished for the comforting words of his mother, but he was too far away to hear her soothing voice.

Comfort—oh, yes, it was for words of comfort and encouragement that his heart was yearning; and, having learned the true source of this fountain, he quickly turned to his Bible. Before opening it he thought, "I will read tonight just where the book happens to open!" and when he looked upon the pages, he saw the name "James" in large letters before him.

Seeing the familiar name of his former friend brought with it a flood of recollections. In imagination, he was once more back near his old home with those boys. James, his companion and teacher, was giving instructions. Instinctively shrinking from these memories, he thought, "I can safely take this other James as my teacher and guide." He began reading at once.

"Blessed is the man that endureth temptation: for when he is tried, he shall receive the crown of life, which the Lord hath promised to them that love him. Let no man say when he is tempted, I am tempted of God: for God cannot be tempted with evil, neither tempteth he any man: But every man is tempted, when he is drawn away of his own lust, and enticed. Then when lust hath conceived, it bringeth forth sin: and sin, when it is finished, bringeth forth death. Do not err, my beloved brethren. Every good gift and every perfect gift is from above, and cometh down from the Father of lights, with whom is no variableness, neither shadow of turning. Of his own will begat he us with the word of truth, that we should be a kind of firstfruits of his creatures. Wherefore, my beloved brethren, let every man be swift to hear, slow to speak, slow to wrath: For the wrath of man worketh not the righteousness of God. Wherefore lay apart all filthiness and superfluity of naughtiness, and receive with meekness the engrafted word, which is able to save your souls. But be ye doers of the word, and not hearers only, deceiving your own selves. For if any be a hearer of the word, and not a doer, he is like unto a man beholding his natural face in a glass: For he beholdeth himself, and goeth his way, and straightway forgetteth what manner of man he was. But whoso looketh into the perfect law of liberty, and continueth therein, he being not a forgetful hearer, but a doer of the work, this man shall be blessed in his deed. If any man among you seem to be religious, and bridleth not his tongue, but deceiveth his own heart, this man's religion is vain. Pure religion and undefiled before God and the Father is this, To visit the fatherless and widows in their affliction, and to keep himself unspotted from the world."

Long after reading this portion of Scripture, Byron sat in deep meditation. It meant more to be a Christian than he had supposed when he started in the Lord's service, but he was glad that the way was daily becoming plainer to him, and that the Lord was so patient with him regarding what he did not know and understand. He did not want to be like the man who, after beholding himself in the mirror, went away and forgot what he was like; he wanted to understand and do the entire will of God and to abide by the instruction obtained from His Word. The book of James he found to be one of his best instructors.

He encountered many trials and tests along the way, but they only drove him closer to his Savior. In earnest supplication he poured out his heart to God in prayer for more strength and ability to win the battles that were ahead of him.

The weekly letters from home were bright spots indeed in his life, and with eagerness and pleasure he looked forward to the days when they were due. Many times while reading about the happenings upon the farm, he felt a degree of homesickness and longed to be back with the loved ones again.

Thus the weeks and months sped by. At the end of the first year he was permitted to return to his former home for a short visit. How good it seemed to be with Mother! How glad he was to sit and hear her talk to him as she used to do! He was as much interested as ever in all the proceedings upon the farm and noted every improvement.

The meetings at the little chapel filled his mind with both pleasant and unpleasant memories. His old friends, eager to know of his new life, inquired of his success, and he was glad to tell them that he was prospering in both soul and body.

When the family gathered around the family altar, Byron realized as never before what his mother's prayers were to him. In bygone days he had grown accustomed to hearing her ask God's blessings upon him, and did not realize the true value of her prayers. While listening to her voice now, he understood as he had never been able to understand before, her earnestness, and why he had so often been blessed while away from her. Her prayers had followed him, and God had heard and answered.

His visit passed all too quickly, and when the time arrived for him to return to his work, he was sorry. But he would be expected at work upon a certain date, so he made arrangements accordingly, and on the day appointed he was at his desk ready for service. Resuming his former duties, he was soon helping to push the business forward with commendable zeal.

Time sped along, and the years rolled by. Now and then Byron made a short visit to his old home. Suddenly he awoke to the fact that his beloved mother was no longer a young woman. She was growing old and rapidly failing in health. One day a letter came saying that his mother was sick, and another the next day said she was no better.

Sorrow settled over Byron's heart like a great darkness. "What if Mother should die?" When he asked himself this question, his courage and strength seemed to fail him. "It would be hard, oh! so hard, to give her up," he thought. "How can I part with her? She has been so much to me!" He hardly dared to think of it and he seemed to be living in constant dread of something that he shrank from forming into words.

He sat at his desk trying to drown his feelings by applying himself diligently to his work. Then a messenger boy entered with an envelope in his hand. With trembling fingers Byron took the envelope from the boy and, finding it addressed to himself, tore it open. The telegram read: "Mother is dangerously sick. Come home at once."

As he had been hoping for favorable news, the message shocked him greatly. Fortunately there was nothing to keep him from going at once, and he was soon on board a train, hastening to her. She might pass away before he reached her bedside, he thought. He pled with God to spare her until he could speak to her once more.

As Byron stepped out on the platform in front of the depot in his home town, he drew his collar higher about his neck, for the wind was blowing and he felt the change from the heated train. His brother was waiting to drive him to the old home at once, and the two hastened away to the carriage. Neither said much as they drove along through the country. Each was busy with his own sad thoughts. Their mother, Byron learned, was somewhat better, but there was little hope of her recovery.

When the old farmhouse came into sight, Byron could scarcely wait and sprang to the group even before the horses had stopped. Hastening to the house, he opened the door and entered. There beside the stove, in her easy chair, sat Mother. It was a happy surprise for Byron to see his mother in her chair and able to greet him. God had answered his prayer, and he learned that her improvement had begun not long after the telegram had been sent.

How the face of that fond mother lighted with smiles as she saw her son hastening toward her and how his heart throbbed with joy as he embraced her frail form! Byron spent the entire day with his mother, and her strength to visit with him was marvelous to all. During the night she slept well and was able to rise again in the morning, but she wanted no breakfast.

"I will stay with you, Mother, while the others eat," Byron said.

When they were alone, she said, "Byron, I wish that you would read to me from the Bible. Please turn to the 103rd Psalm and read."

As Byron read he realized as never before the food and strength contained in the Bible for the Christian. Every word seemed an inspiration; and when he finished the Psalm, he said, "Mother, I never knew before that there was so much in that chapter. It seems to contain just the encouragement that we both need this morning."

"I know it, my son," his mother replied weakly. "It has comforted me many times, but, as you say, I think I have received more courage from the reading of it today than ever before. Isn't the tenth verse marked? Start there and read it to me again."

So Byron read: " 'He hath not dealt with us after our sins; nor rewarded us according to our iniquities. For as the heaven is high above the earth, so great is his mercy toward them that fear him. As far as the east is from the west, so far hath he removed our transgressions from us. Like as a father pitieth his children, so the Lord pitieth them that fear him. For he knoweth our frame; he remembereth that we are dust. As for man, his days are as grass: as a flower of the field, so he flourisheth. For the wind passeth over it, and it is gone; and the place thereof shall know it no more. But the mercy of the Lord is from everlasting to everlasting upon them that fear him, and his righteousness unto children's children; To such as keep his covenant, and to those that remember his commandments to do them. The Lord hath prepared his throne in the heavens; and his kingdom ruleth over all. Bless the Lord, ye his angels, that excel in strength, that do his commandments, hearkening unto the voice of his word. Bless ye the Lord, all ye his hosts; ye ministers of his, that do his pleasure. Bless the Lord, all his works in all places of his dominion: bless the Lord, O my soul.' "

"Do you know, Byron," his mother said, "that if God dealt with us according to our sins He would not only have cut us off from our inheritance, but have blotted our names out of existence and made us worse than the animal kingdom or the flowers and grass of the fields? Instead of this He has pitied us, for He knows how weak we are, and remembers that our frames are dust. If we do well, we shall reign with Him in heaven."

Byron noticed that she seemed very weak, and bowing beside her chair, he prayed, thanking God for sparing her so long. He little realized how very close the death-angel was standing.

"Byron, I've enjoyed our little worship together more than I can tell," she said. "I'm so thankful that I've been spared until you could be with me, but I'm tired now and should like to lie down."

Those were the last words that she ever spoke. Byron helped her to her bed, and she seemed to rest easy. Soon they found that she was unconscious, and in a few hours the summons came. Thus she departed from her loved ones to be with the Savior whom she loved so dearly and who had helped her through so many of the perplexing difficulties of life.

As Byron looked upon the lifeless form of his mother, he noted her noble brow and finely chiseled features. Age and suffering had left their stamp, but there remained the same gentle expression and delicate lines that had marked the strength of her character and the depth of her wisdom. The ashen lips could no longer warn him of danger, but they had directed him to the One who could not only warn him, but pilot his soul into the haven that she had at last entered.